Trail Guide
to
America Online

**A rapid-reading reference to using and cruising the
America Online service**

JONATHAN PRICE

Addison-Wesley Publishing Company
Reading, Massachusetts • Menlo Park, California
New York • Don Mills, Ontario • Wokingham, England
Amsterdam • Bonn • Sydney • Singapore • Tokyo
Madrid • San Juan • Paris • Seoul • Milan
Mexico City • Taipei

Many of the designations used by manufacturers and sellers to distinguish their products are claimed as trademarks. Where those designations appear in this book, and Addison-Wesley was aware of a trademark claim, the designations have been printed in initial capital letters or all capital letters.

The authors and publishers have taken care in preparation of this book, but make no expressed or implied warranty of any kind and assume no responsibility for errors or omissions. No liability is assumed for incidental or consequential damages in connection with or arising out of the use of the information or programs contained herein.

Library of Congress Cataloging-in-Publication Data

Price, Jonathan, 1941–
     The trail guide to America online / Jonathan Price.
          p.   cm.
     Includes index.
     ISBN 0–201–40833–3
     1. America Online (Videotex system) I. Title.
QA76.57.A43P75   1994
004.69—dc20   94–13867
                                                                            CIP

Sponsoring Editor: Claire Horne
Project Manager: Joanne Clapp Fullagar
Production Coordinator: Gail McDonald Jordan
Technical Reviewer: Willow Newmedia Services
Cover design: Barbara T. Atkinson
Text design: Melissa Kulig
Set in 11 point Palatino by NK Graphics

1 2 3 4 5 6 7 8 9-DOH-9897969594
First printing, November 1994

Addison-Wesley books are available for bulk purchases by corporations, institutions, and other organizations. For more information please contact the Corporate, Government and Special Sales Department at (617) 944-3700 x2915.

Dedication

For Lisa, with love

Contents

INTRODUCTION

Why I Wrote This Trail Guide

So you've just signed up with America Online, or you're thinking about it, or you've used it for a while but you feel a bit overwhelmed with all the services offered. If you're like me, you may have had some unsettling experiences.

For instance, you find yourself standing at the edge of a cliff looking out over a forest of icons, all hinting of fascinating activities, ideas, knowledge, and contact with other people—and you freeze. The panorama's so vast, you may wonder which way to turn, what to do next, and, as a result, you stop right there, or just venture out to get your mail and go back home.

Or you set off with a destination in mind, but can't find it. You think you're following all the signs, but, instead of going anywhere, you seem to be circling, slowly, back to where you started. Or, worse, you get stuck in some dead end and can't back out or go forward.

Or you take one path, then another, and another, and pretty soon you can't remember how you got there. You wish you had a clear map of the whole online world so you could figure out where you are.

Perhaps you've changed directions so often you've lost your way. You feel frustrated and anxious, particularly when it occurs to you that you may be wasting your time and money in this twisting trek.

That's why I wrote this trail guide. It puts you in control. You'll feel a lot more confident as you venture into these new territories because I give you step-by-step advice on how to get around. And you'll spot the areas you want to go into next because I lay out a map of the service, from A (the *Atlantic Monthly* forum) to Z (*Zebras* in the encyclopedia).

This guide offers you three main sections: a brief overview of America Online at the beginning, a set of how-to's for everything you're likely to want to do online, and then a survey of what's out there on the service for you to explore.

- If you're new to the whole idea of networks and information services, turn to Part I to find out how America Online outshines the rest. (You'll learn how to sign on, too.)

- If you want to know how to do something, look the task up in Part II.

- If you're curious about what kind of people, ideas, services, or surprises are waiting for you out there in parts of the service you have never set foot in, browse through Part III.

You'll learn the lay of the land, begin to pioneer new areas, develop confidence in various shortcuts, and, most important, develop a mental picture of the way each piece of this gigantic puzzle fits together. Gradually, you'll find you can more easily retrace your steps, recognizing landmarks along the way, perhaps even learning a few magic charms by heart, and, almost without noticing it, making sense out of all of these experiences.

You'll be doing what you hoped to when you signed up:

- Swapping stories, ideas, and advice with other people who are interested in the same hobbies, products, issues.

- Picking up a lot of useful software, drawings, photographs, videos, sample files, and raw information.

- Investigating fields of expertise you never even imagined existed, getting a glimpse of the way very different people think, all without leaving your desk.

- Learning, learning, learning. Learning in online courses; looking up facts in the various huge files of newspaper articles, encyclopedia entries, statistics, charts, and listings.

- Striking up a conversation with an invisible but very lively person who may live halfway across the continent.

- Sending letters, receiving them, and trading whole documents with other people.

- Tapping into the super-network known as Internet to collect hundreds of pages of information every day from the hundreds of thousands of special interest groups around the globe; looking up books in the Sydney, Australia library; or collecting on-the-spot messages from people in the midst of natural disasters or civil war.

Conventions in This Book

I've used icons in the book to flag particular items or entries for special notice. Here's what they look like, and what they mean:

This icon marks a useful and informative tip on what to do (or what not to do) under certain circumstances.

This icon marks background information, America Online trivia, or other esoterica. While some people may find this stuff perfectly fascinating, you shouldn't feel obligated to read it. If you like, you can skip these sections without missing any crucial information.

 This icon marks a method for getting things done more quickly or efficiently. If you're interested in attaining power-user status on America Online, you'll probably want to check out these items.

Arriving at Your Destination

When you've used this trail guide, off and on, for a while, I think that you will feel that you know your way around all of America Online. You'll understand the basic terrain, so even when the seasons change, and services come and go, you'll know how to get to the old watering holes, clusters of civilization, or outposts—and back home. You'll meet a lot more people because you'll be able to make contact with so many more exciting events, lectures, conferences, and venues for exchanges of opinion. You'll be able to explore unfamiliar areas without anxiety because you'll know, basically, how America Online works. And you'll take part in the dozens of late-breaking events popping up all across America Online.

PART **I**

STARTING AMERICA ONLINE

If you're not sure what you're getting into with America Online, this is the part for you. You'll get an eagle's view of the whole place in Chapter One. Then, if you want to sign on for the first time, you'll find out how, in Chapter Two.

If you've already signed on, and want to know more about the activities you can try out online, please turn to Part II, Exploring America Online.

And if you'd like to know what kind of information you'll find where, please turn to Part III, What You'll Find Online.

CHAPTER **1**

WELCOME TO AMERICA ONLINE

Like a national park, America Online stretches over hundreds of miles of trails, through small communities, scenic overlooks, crowded avenues, and more than a thousand special places. Visiting, you get a sense of the sprawling variety of people and societies that make up the United States—bicyclers, photographers, travelers, hunters, hikers, car nuts, airplane fanatics, political gossips, oh, and even a vice president.

Getting Together

You talk to folks on the phone, you write them letters, you chat over lunch. Well, with America Online, you get to swap stories with people in a new way. You meet people you'd never run into down at the mall; you find out what they think; and, cloaked in a little anonymity, knowing they probably won't ever meet you, or know anything about you beyond what you say, you have a chance to talk with strangers. You type a sentence or two, and someone else replies, and maybe another person with a "handle" like Lamp33 gives you advice. At once obscure and open, these conversations expand your horizon—you bump into people who hugely disagree with you, others who are potential friends, and still others who are as obsessed as you with some small subject like stamps.

America Online provides the imaginary spaces in which we can chat, a very fast mail service to send letters back and forth, and public bulletin boards on which we can post our ideas and get responses from others. Hundreds of associations have their own chat rooms and boards so you can ask their staffs for ideas, read their position papers, and get details on current issues.

Getting Information

On America Online there aren't very many books, but there are a million statistics; articles from dozens of magazines; data sheets on thousands of products; listings of every commercial airline flight in America; registration information about thousands of hotel rooms; schedules of TV shows, art shows, discussions, and annual meetings; and so many facts, facts, facts that if you printed them all out, one to a page, you could fill your local library.

You can look it up. Ask the *National Geographic* about Wales. See what the encyclopedia has to say about whales. Check the bio of a rock wailer or the special codes of a video game. Until you explore America Online, you may never have realized how many facts there are out there!

It's a library, a newsstand, a museum. You won't find everything there, but it sure beats the *Farmers' Almanac*.

Shopping

You know how you can dial up one of those 800 numbers on TV and order a special mattress delivered direct from the factory? Well, America Online's not as full of commercials as TV, but you can buy books; order flowers; reserve flights, cars, and hotel rooms; and purchase computers, stereos, dishwashers, videotapes, CDs, and magazine subscriptions. So why buy this way?

The biggest reason is if you know what you want, you're likely to pay less. But the darndest thing is it seems more convenient. You just sit at your desk, type a few numbers, and in a day or so, the package arrives!

All on Top of Your Desk

At first, chatting, learning, and shopping like this seems odd. After all, you haven't driven to the mall, waited for the library to open, or spent a half-hour trying to sidle up next to someone at a party. You're using your keyboard. You're looking at the same screen you've surrounded with yellow stickies.

Suddenly your computer can do so much more than word processing and budgeting. These windows show more than numbers and letters.

You run an application on your own computer—a program called America Online. The program lets you reach out along the phone lines to talk to a giant computer, called the host. The host runs some other software that lets you send mail, chat, and buy. The whole setup—from your computer to theirs, and back—is also known as America Online.

The great thing about AOL (shorthand for America Online) is that you don't have to worry about the complex and unpredictable realm of telecommunications. Remember when you bought the modem in your computer? It probably came with some software with a name like Magic Whizbang TeleComm, a manual that's virtually meaningless, and ten switches you don't understand. AOL shields you from the ugly settings that establish connection.

But the best thing about America Online is not its software or computers, amazing as they are; it's the people who staff the forums. The customer support folks who help you right when you need it. The hosts who show you around the chat rooms. The leaders who answer your questions and show newcomers around.

What's Unique about America Online

Three pleasures make America Online stand out from other information services you can dial into.

- The way the software shows you what you can do. You don't have to guess. You don't have to remember obscure commands, or understand exactly where some file is in a dense directory of oddly named thingamabobs. You see an icon, with a name under it, you click it, and you go right there. There's plenty of help available. The *interface*—the look of the screen, the buttons, the whole way you interact with the program— opens the way for you.

- The presence of other people, right there when you are there, makes the conversations interesting, whether you're joining in or just "listening." You get so many responses to a question on a bulletin board, you know you're not alone in your interest. And we're talking rapid fire. Just while you're signed on, you may get new mail. That means a lot of interaction with other people through this unusual medium.

- So many people dial in every day that nothing stays the same for long. Your questions get answered, new people charge into your chat room, mail keeps dropping into your mailbox. New forums open up every week. New games. New activities. New hobbies. You find yourself coming back just to see what's appeared.

In the next chapter I'll describe your first time on America Online. Then in Part II I'll give you step-by-step instructions on how to use the services; Part III provides an in-depth guided tour of the whole environment.

CHAPTER **2**

GETTING STARTED

In this chapter you'll find out how to get ready, get set, and go on America Online. If you've already signed up and made the connection, you don't need to read this chapter—please jump to Part II, which tells you how to do almost everything you can do online, or Part III, which takes you on an extensive tour of every department so you know what's waiting for you out there. If you're about to sign on, be sure to flip to the back of the book for a special coupon; use it to get the sign-on software, and some free time online, if you don't already have the America Online disk.

What You Need

To take advantage of the amazing world of AOL, you can use a DOS PC, a Windows PC with Windows 3.1 or later, an Apple II, any Macintosh from the Plus on, or an Atari. Your computer should have a few megabytes of hard disk space free to store all the AOL software and files. And then you'll also need . . .

A Modem and a Phone Line

The modem takes the on and off signals, or bits, coming out of your computer and translates them into the undulating waves of sound that your average phone line can pass along. The translation is called **modulating** when you are sending a message, and then, at the other end, when the message comes in from the phone lines, **demodulating,** so another computer can make sense of the message.

Modems send out information at different speeds, measured in bits per second (bps), or baud. (Not every bit is meaningful to us humans; there are extra bits thrown in to test to make sure your message is going through correctly.) The faster your modem communicates, the more information you can send and receive in a second—and when you want to download a big color picture, that can make the difference between a short pause and a long wait. You can communicate with AOL at 2400 baud or 9600 baud.

Your modem may be built into your computer, or it may sit in a separate box with its own blinking lights. In either case, it has a cable receiving information from the computer, another going out to a phone jack (the squarish hole in the wall, with a little extra notch where the plastic flap at the end of your cable snaps into place), and another to pass along the phone signal to your telephone handset, if you want to use it on this line.

In the best of circumstances, you have a phone line you can dedicate to electronic communication, so your fax machine and your modem can share it. If you are sending a message on your modem, and a fax comes in, the sender just gets a signal that your line is busy. If you receive a fax when you aren't using your modem, the fax machine picks up. And nobody calls in, you hope, because if they do, they may hear the warbling whistles and beeps of the fax or modem at work.

Second best is a regular line out of your house. The problem: What if someone else wants to make a call while you are using the phone line to get in touch with America Online? You may have to quit quickly. Or you may set up an automatic dial-in to collect your mail late at night, called a FlashSession, so you aren't interfering with incoming or outgoing calls.

 You can split your phone line for less than $5. Go to a phone or electronics store and get a splitter; it plugs into a single phone jack in the wall and offers two jacks. Plug your phone into one and your modem into the other. Then incoming calls will go to your phone, and your callers won't get screeched at.

Worst is a line that goes out through a switchboard, such as a hotel or business. You can use this kind of line, but you'll probably have to tinker with the setup in the software. For instance, you may have to dial 9 to get an outside line, and you'll need to tell the software to do that, then wait five seconds before proceeding to dial the outside number.

The Software

America Online makes it very simple to sign up. It distributes starter kits with magazines and modems, on some manufacturers' hard disks, and on CD-ROM. AOL is glad to mail you one if you call them: 800-827-6364.

The starter kit comes with a disk and a certificate. Here's what to do with them:

1. **Make a copy of the starter disk, as a backup.**
2. **Make sure you have 2 megabytes of room on your hard disk, and at least 700K of RAM available above what's needed for your operating system.**
3. **Put the copy of your AOL disk into the drive.**
4. **Run the installer program.**

   On the Macintosh, just double-click the Installer icon, and tell it where to put the files.

On Windows, go to the Program Manager, and on the File menu choose Run and type A:Install (where A is your floppy drive) and press Return. When welcomed, click Continue. The installer suggests setting up a directory on your hard disk called WAOL. If you want to put it somewhere else, type the drive letter and full path (directory and any subdirectories) to the spot you want to put the files. Click Continue.

5. **Take a look at the files that have been installed.**

They take up a lot more room than they did on the floppy disk, because the installer unzipped them using PKZIP, StuffIt, or some other compression software.

How to Sign Up for the First Time

Now that you have the software installed and your hardware hooked up, you can dial in to become a member. The first session takes 10 or 15 minutes, during which you answer a bunch of questions, and, if necessary, straighten out the connection.

1. **Start the America Online software and pass the Welcome screen to one dense with text that lists the assumptions AOL has made about your situation.**

They assume that you are using a touch-tone phone, you have your modem connected, you don't need to dial 9 to get an outside line, you don't have call waiting (which can disrupt your connection), and, possibly, you are calling from the continental United States.

2. **If you live in Canada, have a rotary phone, or have to dial 9, click Options, fill in the blanks, and then click OK.**

An old-fashioned rotary phone issues signals as pulses, not tones, so choose Pulse.

If you need to dial 9, put in a 9, and then a comma for each second you have to wait before dialing the outside number.

When you finish filling out the options and click OK, the software does some internal checking. (Can it find the modem? How fast can it send signals out?)

3. **Click OK or Continue to sign on.**

The software dials an 800 number. If your modem has a speaker, you should hear the dial tone and then the numbers being dialed very quickly. Then you should hear a low continuous screeching, as your modem links up with the 800 number's modem. Then there should be more beeps and clicks, and you see a welcome from the AOL host computers.

- If you don't hear a dial tone, the problem is likely to be in your setup. Check to make sure all cables are in and that the modem's on and firmly attached to the computer.

- If you don't hear the screeching, try connecting again in a few moments because the problem may be that the network is not responding.

- If you get past the screeching, and then fail, the problem may be anywhere along the chain. Try one or two more times.

- If all these attempts fail, call AOL Customer Service at 800-827-6364. You might expect a long wait and a surly response, but even when busy, these folks are different. They have long lists of the 1,001 modems people use, and they know many things that can go wrong; they can talk you through redoing your software setup, or hardware connection, so that you can sign on.

Setting Up Your Account

Now that you're connected, you need to pick a local access number—the phone number you'll call from now on. You're asked to type in your area code, and AOL looks that up and comes back with a list of nearby numbers. You pick one as your first choice, and another as your second choice.

(If the first number does not answer, AOL tries the other automatically.) These numbers connect you to a network that picks up your call, and in most cases zips it over a satellite to get to the AOL computers in Virginia.

 Note the column that shows how fast each line is. Pick the fastest one your modem can handle. If your modem works faster than those speeds, pick the fastest one available. Later, when you're through with all the paperwork, go to Members' Online Support and look for a list of 9600 baud access numbers, or higher.

When you finish entering the two phone numbers, AOL disconnects you from the 800 number and dials your first choice. You're greeted this time with a request for the number of your certificate, and the password shown on the certificate. (Use the Tab key to move from one to the next, then click Continue.)

Now you're asked for your name, address, and phone number, so they can reach you at home if something goes wrong. (They hardly ever call.)

Next comes money. You can't pay AOL directly; you have to use VISA, MasterCard, Discover, Amex, or a bank debit card; AOL bills the card directly, and you see a monthly entry, usually at a rate of $10 for five hours.

And now you get to create a screen name—the name most other people will know you by when you sign on. Try to be more expressive than the name AOL suggests for you: they suggested I call myself Jon4555, meaning I was the 4,555th Jon to sign on. Be sure to Select Alternate. You may have to choose several alternates, because with almost a million people online, a lot of the good monikers have been chosen.

Then you need to type a password of at least four characters, but no more than eight. If there is any chance that someone else might use your machine without your permission, do not make it easy for them to guess. Not recommended as passwords: your first name, your middle name, your last name, your spouse's name, your dog's name, your child's name, your birthday.

When you type your password, you'll only see asterisks onscreen. That's so nosy folks leaning over your shoulder can't tell what your password is.

Reading a Letter from Steve Case

Almost as soon as you sign on, someone sends you mail. It's the president of America Online!

1. **Choose Read New Mail from the Mail menu.**

    You'll see that you have a message from Steve Case. It is highlighted.

2. **Click the Read button.**

3. **If you want to respond, click Reply and write the letter.**

    AOL knows where to send your reply, because it brought you the original; you don't have to fill in an address.

Wandering

You have some free time coming to you as a new member. Take advantage of it and just explore.

- For instance, if you are using Windows, click the icons in the Flashbar to see what department each one takes you to.

- If you are using a Macintosh, choose to take the tour, or click the Departments button, and then keep on clicking.

PART **II**

Exploring America Online

If you want to know more about what you can actually do online, this part is for you. You'll find step-by-step instructions for signing on, moving around, getting help, and dozens of other fascinating activities.

You might think of this part as a miniature manual for America Online. The people at America Online are convinced that you'll find everything you need to know just by clicking on this or that icon, so they have never put out a manual. But in talking with friends, I've found that first-time users can feel a little intimidated by the profusion of icons, commands, levels, and places to go. Exciting as the online world can be, it's also confusing.

That's why I've built this part of the book around procedures—each with its own heading, introduction, and series of numbered steps. For extras, I've thrown in plenty of tips. I'm hoping that you'll try out some of the activities you may have heard about, but never tried, because you weren't sure how to play.

If you're a beginner, and uncertain about how to get around, please turn to Chapter 3.

If you want to know how to send and receive mail, exchange messages with other people who are online at the same time you are, and even collect neat utilities or files, read Chapter 4.

If you like to play games or participate in live events, please read Chapter 5.

If you want to look up facts, take a course, get help with your homework, or plan for college, please turn to Chapter 6.

And finally, if you just like conversation, you can start typing instead of talking, and join dozens of live discussions, doing what onliners call "chatting," described in Chapter 7.

So this whole part of the book is about going places and doing things. Look up whatever you need, or browse through a few pages here and there, to get an idea of what new excitement you can participate in.

Then, to learn exactly what kind of information you'll find where, please turn to Part III, What You'll Find Online.

CHAPTER **3**

SIGNING ON AND OFF, MOVING AROUND, AND GETTING HELP

Getting out of the house, even though it's over the phone lines, plunges you into the online world. You must navigate from point to point, with or without a compass, occasionally asking for a little support from a guide, but mostly exploring on your own. At first, just as when you go to a neighborhood park, you have a tendency to follow the familiar paths, checking on the flowers and trees you've seen before, but rarely striking out into new territory. Online, you may be similarly timid about ranging freely because you don't know what's out there, you aren't sure of the shortcuts, and you worry about getting back if you don't like what you find.

In this chapter, you'll learn how to sign on, browse around, and, if you need help, how to get it in half-a-dozen forms. Even though the online world is huge, you'll develop confidence that you can jump from one end to the other, electronically. Alley oop!

Signing On and Off and Quitting

 Here's a quick glimpse of the process: you turn on your America Online software, and then you sign on to a network that connects your personal computer to the host computer at America Online's headquarters in Virginia. Keep in mind that when you sign on, you are making a connection—over the phone lines—to at least one, and possibly a whole set of very big computers, sending messages to them, and receiving, in return, tons of information. Later, when you sign off, you drop that connection. But your software is still active, so you can perform some housekeeping chores using your own computer, without having to pay for any more connect time than necessary. Finally, when you're done with those chores, you quit the application on your desktop computer.

Signing On

The first time you sign on, you're guided through the process by the software. After that, you're a regular, and the whole process of signing on goes quickly, because most of it is done for you while you watch. Here's how to sign on, as a regular.

1. **Double-click your America Online application to launch it.**

   You see the sign-on window, with your user name already in place. This doesn't have to be your real name—it's just the name you give out to the rest of the online world. In the world of Citizen Band radio, this would be known as your "handle" (Figure 3.1).

2. **Type your password.**

   To make sure nobody can read the password over your shoulder—and sign on when you're not looking—the password appears as a series of asterisks.

Figure 3.1   *Welcome*

3. **Click Sign On.**

A window appears, reporting on the progress of your call. You'll see several technical phrases that you can ignore—stuff like, "Opening connect file," which means the program is looking up information such as what number to call; "Initializing modem," which means it's getting the modem ready to send information over the phone lines; and "Dialing" and "Accessing the network," which mean the program has reached the special network that will carry your call to America Online.

Occasionally, America Online will interrupt your sign-on by sending you a new piece of art, or an icon. These graphics are stored with your application on your hard disk, to eliminate the expense and time it would otherwise take to send them to you every time you signed on. From now on, whenever you go to a department represented by any of these icons, your software draws the image from your disk, which is fast, rather than receiving it again over the phone lines, which could be slow. Clever, huh?

Finally, if your computer has sound, and the volume's turned up, you hear a voice saying, "Welcome!" You see a welcome screen *somewhat* like the one shown in Figure 3.2. (The right-hand side changes every day, advertising new services and special events.)

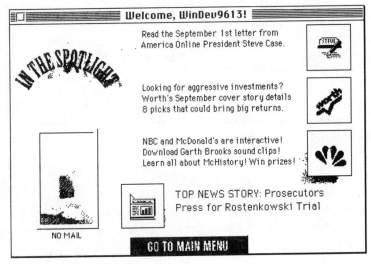

Figure 3.2 *You've arrived!*

4. Go wherever.

- Click Go to Main Menu, then click Discover AOL.
- If the Mail icon shows you have mail, and you want to

read that now, click the icon on the left (the hand holding up your mail).

- To go directly to one of the featured services or events on the right, just click its icon.
- To go to a window displaying all the departments, click Go to Main Menu, at the bottom.

You can also use the Go To menu, as we'll describe in the next section, "Moving Around."

Signing Off

Signing off is like hanging up the phone after a conversation. It doesn't turn off your software; it just drops your electronic tie to the giant computers of America Online in Virginia.

1. On the Go To menu choose Sign Off.

This command disconnects you from the network. You're still using the America Online application on your own computer, but your connection to the mainframe computers run by America Online has been broken. You are no longer being charged for the connection.

Signing off this way makes sure that the host computers—those big ones in Virginia—recognize that you have left.

Breaking the connection the wrong way—by turning off your computer or modem while you are still connected to America Online's computers—runs the risk of allowing them to think you are still connected, and then charging you for hours and hours of time. (Of course, eventually their software detects that there is no signal on the line, and they recognize that you have dropped out of sight. But that might take a half-hour or so, during which time you're still being charged for your connection time.)

Signing off is not the same as quitting the application. That's still running. You can now use the software to reread mail, or change your setup—activities for which you don't need to be connected to the host computers.

If you want to sign off and quit all at once, choose Quit from the File menu. You'll be asked if you really want to quit, or just sign off. Click Quit, to do both.

Working Offline

When you're offline, whatever you see on your screen comes from some kind of disk (floppy, hard, CD, optical, whatever) attached directly to your own computer. You have no link to the vast open spaces of the online world. That's OK. It's quiet. You can get a little work done.

1. **If you are launching America Online, choose Setup in the dialog box, or use the menu options to start one of the following tasks:**

- Writing a note—choose Compose Mail from the Mail menu.

- Modifying your address book—choose Edit Address Book from the Mail menu.

- Changing something in your Setup, such as the phone number you call to reach America Online—click Setup in the dialog box, or choose Setup and Sign On from the Go To menu, and then click Setup.

- Starting a Flash Session—Now, choose Activate Flash-Session from the Mail menu and click Go Ahead in the next dialog. (In a FlashSession you have the computer sign on, collect your mail, and sign off, as quickly as it can, to save time.)

- Setting up the way you want to carry out chats, send and receive mail, display text onscreen, and identify yourself to other members—choose Set Preferences from the Members menu.

2. **If you are connected to the host computers and decide you want to carry out one of those tasks without using live information from America Online, choose Sign Off from the Go To menu.**

You are disconnected from the host computer. You can now use the commands on the menus. (Of course, any commands that apply only to work online appear dimmed, because they are not available.)

Quitting

Quitting the America Online application puts the whole program away.

1. **Choose Quit from the File menu.**

   If you have been working offline (that is, not connected via the phone lines to the host computer in Virginia), you see any open AOL windows close. If you have been working on a document but have not saved it, you get a chance to save your work. And then, after a pause, the menu bar goes away. That's it.

   If you're connected to the host computer when you choose Quit, you're presented with a dialog box that asks you to confirm that you really want to quit, as opposed to just signing off (while keeping the program active on your own computer). Click Quit.

   You're notified when the application drops its connection with the host computer (signing off), and then you see the sign-on window for a few moments. Depending on the speed of your computer, you may feel as if you have to take some additional action after signing off, because the application takes so long putting all its pieces away. You don't. Just wait. Eventually the sign-on window—and any other AOL windows—disappear.

Moving Around

Exploring the electronic world of America Online is a lot easier than hiking the Appalachian Trail. You issue a command, and presto! You're there.

And you have your choice of several ways to issue those commands: You can jump from icon to icon, you can press a button, you can choose a command from a menu, or you can type a keyword to go directly to a particular location. Once there, you may need to scroll up and down—this is the heavy work—and, gosh, sometimes you may even have to double-click to see the contents of a directory. But the effort's nothing like backpacking a hundred pounds of canned goods up a rocky streambed.

Using Icons and Buttons

America Online offers two kinds of icons for moving about. Some are fully detailed little paintings, often with several colors, presenting a texture or something in the real world, such as an airplane, or people chatting (Figure 3.3). Built into the art is a label, usually the name of some location, such as a bulletin board or department.

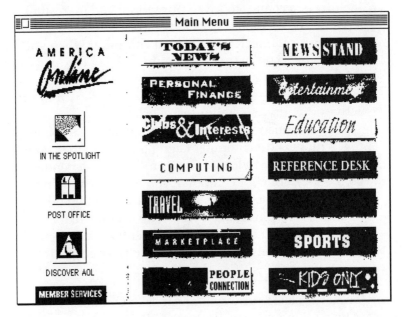

Figure 3.3 *The Main menu with the departments on the right*

- **To go to the location represented by the color-sketch icon (and named in the label) click the icon. (Once should do it.)**

Another window opens, in front of the window you were just in.

Other icons are those plainer line-drawings supplied by your operating system, representing documents or directories (folders full of documents). When double-clicked, these plain-jane drawings simply open to reveal lists of files—or individual documents.

- **To open a document or directory represented by one of the system icons, double-click the icon.**

A window containing the list of files, or the document itself, opens in front of the window you were just in.

 A good rule of thumb: Click the icon. Wait a few seconds to see if something happens. If absolutely nothing happens during four or five seconds, double-click the icon.

Buttons also advertise other locations, other windows. The button, though, has no drawing. You are just looking at a name in an oval.

- **To go to the location advertised in the button, click the button.**

A window opens showing the environment of that new location, in front of the window you were just in.

Using Go To Commands

The Go To menu offers a lot of commands that let you jump from mountain to mountain in America Online. Once you've seen all the sights in the valleys and foothills along the way, you'll take more advantage of these direct routes. They take you to:

- A window showing all the major departments, the post office, a tour, and a special event (Main menu)
- A list of major services offered (Search Directory of Services)
- A way to find software (Search Softmail Libraries)

- The latest news about the network (Network News)
- The amount of time you have spent so far during this session (Online Clock)
- Particular locations that you or AOL have placed on the Go To menu, such as New Services (there's always another one), the tour of AOL, Sign on a Friend, the Lobby (where you meet people you might want to chat with), Top News, Stock Quotes, big events on Center Stage, and the Internet Center, for a connection to the biggest net of all

Going to New Services

You can get a list of recent additions to America Online, then go to any that look interesting.

1. Choose New Services on the Go To menu.

If you've inadvertently deleted that option from the Go To menu, choose Keyword from the Go To menu, and enter New.

You get a list of new features and services.

2. Double-click any service that looks interesting.

Going to the People Connection

This is the piazza, where you get to chat with people all around the world, real time.

1. Choose Lobby on the Go To menu.

Or, in Windows, click the People icon on the Flashbar.

2. To see some pictures of the people who are online at this time, click PC (People Connection Studio), and explore.

3. To see what's going on in various chat rooms, click Rooms.

4. To find out who's hanging around the Lobby, click People.

5. For big events, click Center Stage.

6. To block your child's access to certain areas, click Parental Control.

Adding a Destination to the Go To Menu

You can add your own options to the Go To menu—places you want to go back to over and over. Putting a destination on the Go To menu lets you get there in one click, rather than the dozen or more clicks you might need if you were using buttons or icons to move through the peaks and valleys. Here's how to add a location to the Go To menu:

1. **Make your way to the location using any navigation tools you need to—icons, buttons, commands, or whatever.**

2. **When you arrive, note the Keyword at the bottom of the window.**

   Each major location has its own Keyword. You can use the Keyword to go directly to the location, rather than meandering there by clicking and pointing.

3. **Reach up to the Go To menu, and choose Edit Favorite Places.**

   You see a table (Figure 3.4). On the left are the commands you can place on the menu itself; and on the right, the Keywords.

4. **Put the location's name on the menu (on the left) and put the Keyword on the right.**

   You can only use these ten slots. When naming the location on the right, you're free to call it whatever you want. Just make sure you'll remember your own term, later, if you aren't using the standard name.

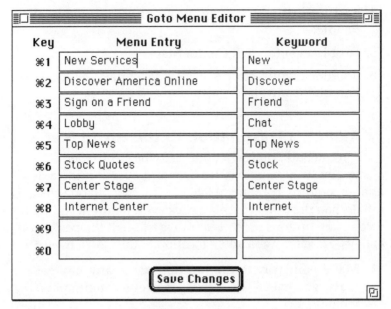

Figure 3.4   *Adding favorite places to the Go to menu*

Zipping Directly to a Window

When you have opened a bunch of windows, and poked around in a lot of locations, your screen becomes a clutter of windows overlaying windows. But the names of all the windows you now have open appear on the Windows menu.

1. **To go directly to an open window, choose its name on the Windows menu. (Or, if you see part of the window, click it to make it active, and bring it to the front.)**

    If the window you want is not listed on the Windows menu, pick one that's close. (You may have inadvertently closed a window as you moved around.) You can then back up, or go forward to the window you're after.

Dialog boxes, in which you must fill out information before AOL can carry out a command, do not count as windows, and do not show up on the list. That makes sense, because you usually have to complete the dialog and close the dialog box before going on. And the menu only lists gizmos that are open.

2. **On the Macintosh, to get rid of every window except the one you're looking at, choose Close All Except Front from the Windows menu; or if you just want to straighten things up, choose Clean Up Windows.**

3. **In Windows, to stack windows like a deck of cards, choose Cascade; to give each its own space, choose Tile.**

Using the Keyboard to Issue Commands

Look next to many of the commands on the menus, including the ones you yourself have added to the Go To menu, and you'll see that there are keyboard shortcuts for some commands. Instead of reaching up and selecting a command, and then clicking the mouse to issue it, you can type the two keys at once to issue the command. If you are a veteran typist, these keystroke combinations speed things up.

If you're using a Macintosh, here are the commands you can issue by pressing two keys at once. The first key is the Command key—it has an Apple on it, and a weird symbol that looks like a butterfly doing loops (⌘).

Help	Command-/
File New Memo	Command-N
File Open	Command-O
File Close	Command-W
File Save	Command-S
File Print	Command-P
File Quit	Command-Q
Edit Undo	Command-Z
Edit Cut	Command-X

Edit Copy	Command-C
Edit Paste	Command-V
Edit Select All	Command-A
Edit Duplicate	Command-D
Go To Keyword	Command-K
Go To Lobby	Command-4
Mail Compose Mail	Command-M
Mail Read New Mail	Command-R
Member Send Instant Message	Command-I
Member Get Member Profile	Command-G
Member Locate a Member Online	Command-F
Member Set Preferences	Command-=

If you're using Windows, you can issue any menu command using the keyboard. To open the menu, press Alt at the same time as the underlined letter in the menu title; the list of commands comes down, and one of them has a rectangular highlight on it. Use the arrow keys to move the highlighting up or down to the option you want, and then press Enter. Or, once the menu is open, just press the underlined letter in the command.

In Windows, the keyboard shortcuts use Control to bypass the process of opening the menu and issuing the command. Here are the shortcuts in the order they appear on menus:

Control Close a Window	Alt-F4
Control Task List	Control-Esc
File New	Control-N
File Open	Control-O
File Save	Control-S
File Print	Control-P
File Download Manager	Control-T
File Stop Incoming Text	Esc
Edit Undo	Control-Z
Edit Cut	Control-X
Edit Copy	Control-C
Edit Paste	Control-V

Edit Select All	Control-A
Go To Main menu	Control-D
Go To Keyword	Control-K
Go To Lobby	Control-L
Go To Personal Items	Control-1 ... 0
Mail Compose Mail	Control-M
Mail Read New Mail	Control-R
Members Send Instant Message	Control-I
Members Get a Member's Profile	Control-G
Members Locate a Member Online	Control-F
Members Set Preferences	Control-=

In Windows, take advantage of the Flashbar. At first, the number of unfamiliar icons seems dizzying, but experiment, and you'll begin to use these shortcuts. Like everything else on America Online, these buttons change over time. But here are some important ones:

- If the flag's up on your mailbox, click the first icon to read new mail.

- To write a letter, click the second icon (showing a pen on top of a letter).

- To go to various locations, click the icons—the Main menu (next to the pen and paper), Member Services (the question mark that looks liks a key), Search Directory of Services (the magnifying glass), or People Connection (the talking heads).

- To save the contents of the front window, click the last icon, showing a document being slipped into a folder.

- To print the contents of the front window, click the next to the last icon, which shows paper emerging from a printer.

Using Keywords to Go Direct

Keywords let you zip right past all kinds of intervening windows to land directly at the spot you want. Any location worth going to has its own Keyword. So if you like a particular area, and think you want to go back, note its Keyword before leaving. (The Keyword often appears in the lower-left corner of a window.)

1. **Choose Keyword from the Go To menu.**
2. **Enter your Keyword and click OK or Go.**

   You go directly to that area.

Looking Up a Keyword

Yes, sometimes you forget. You've tried all the words you can think of and gotten nowhere—or worse, you've ended up on trails you've never seen before. But there's hope. Like pulling a compass out of your pocket, you can look up the keyword.

1. **Choose Keyword from the Go To menu.**

   You see a list of the major departments.

2. **On the Mac, click Keyword Help, choose a Department, and browse through the keywords in that department.**

   In Windows, type a word that is close to what you want, click Search, and (you hope) pick the right keyword from the list presented..

 You can select a keyword, and copy it into your computer's memory, using the Copy command from the Edit menu. Then, when you've returned to the Keyword dialog box, you can insert that into the entry box by choosing Paste from the Edit menu. Copying this way guarantees you won't make any typos. But remember, copy only one keyword. AOL doesn't recognize "career, careers" as a single keyword, and balks until you erase one or the other.

You can also get to the list of keywords by choosing Search Directory of Services from the Go To menu. A list of options appears—one of these is Keywords. Choose Keywords, and you see a list of departments; choose a department, and you see the services in that department, along with their keywords. The lists are the same that you reach through the Keyword dialog box. The Directory simply offers you another path to them.

Using the Directory of Services

You can locate a particular service in the Directory of Services and then go right to it.

1. **Choose Search Directory of Services from the Go To menu.**

2. **In the dialog box, double-click Search the Directory of Services.**

   You see a dialog box asking you to enter a subject (Figure 3.5).

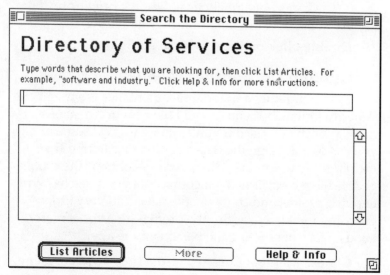

Figure 3.5   *Searching for a service*

3. **If you know the name of the service, type that in. If not, type a keyword, or any word that you think might appear in a description of the service. Then click List Articles.**

   The database searches for the topic you have just typed in, looking through the records for every service. On each service's record are fields containing that service's name, keywords, other words someone might associate with the service (Search words), menu path (the directories you have to go through to get to it), and a detailed description. Given all that information, you're likely to stumble on the right service, along with several similar ones.

   In a few moments, you see a list of the services whose records happen to contain one or more of the words you typed in.

4. **Scroll through the list. To see even more services, click the More button underneath the list.**

   The list is not alphabetical. Best we can figure, the services appear in the order they joined AOL.

5. **Double-click on the service to go right to it.**

Looking Up Another Member

If you think that a friend or acquaintance is a member of America Online but you do not know his or her screen name (which you need if you're going to send some mail), you can leaf through the member directory to find that member's screen name. This directory contains the profiles people have contributed. Of course, not everyone has written up a profile, and some people have said very little, guarding their privacy. But the profiles give you a pretty good chance of spotting the person you're after.

1. **Choose Member Directory from the Members menu.**

2. **In the scrolling list that appears, choose Search the Member Directory.**

You see this Dialog box (Figure 3.6).

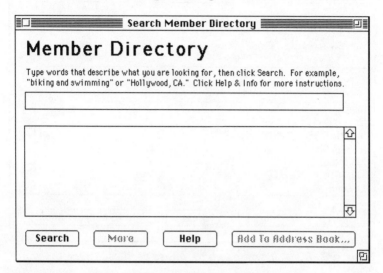

Figure 3.6   *Search Member Directory dialog box*

3. **In the dialog box, type a word or two that you think might appear in the member's profile.**

- Make sure you've spelled the words right.
- Make sure each word contains at least three letters.
- If you don't know how to spell part of a word, or if you want to search for various forms of the word, put an asterisk (*) in place of one or more letters, or a question mark (?) in place of one letter.
- Spaces count. Make sure you have spaces where you mean to. AOL interprets "horses riding" as meaning that you want to find members whose profiles include both words. If you type "horseriding" AOL will look for any profiles that contain that as a single word.

4. **Click Search.**

If you're lucky, you see a list of screen names (Figure 3.7). Double-click one to see the member's profile. You

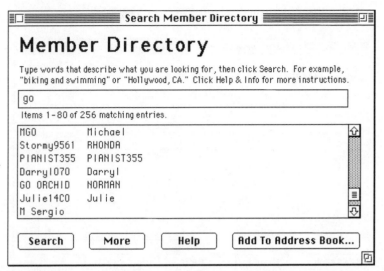

Figure 3.7   *A list of members whose profiles include the word "Go"*

have to read each one to find out whether the person plays the game Go.

If you're not so lucky, you may get no list at all, or a very short list, with no likely names on it. You need to revise or widen your search. Think of several words that might appear in the member's profile, and put OR between them—meaning that you want any profile that contains one or another of those words. Example: Beethoven or Bach.

On the other hand, your first try may have netted so many possible names that AOL asks you to narrow the field a little. If there are two terms you are sure would both appear in the profile you're after, include them with an AND in between. Example: Hollywood AND California. Or, if you want to rule out some folks, use a NOT, like this: Hollywood NOT Ohio.

Don't get too fancy with these Boolean expressions (AND, OR, NOT) because a complex search request can just overwhelm the system, and it gives up.

Looking Up a Member's Profile

If you're curious about another member whose screen name you've run into, you can look up the person's profile—if there is one. (Some people don't contribute a profile.)

1. **Choose Get Member's Profile from the Members menu (Figure 3.8).**

Figure 3.8   *Getting a member's profile*

2. **Enter the person's screen name and click OK.**

   You see the profile, if there is one (Figure 3.9).

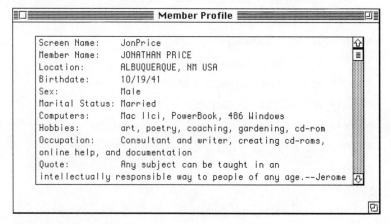

Figure 3.9   *A member's profile*

Locating Someone Who's Online

If you want to locate a member you think is currently
using the system, perhaps to join in a chat, you can find out
where that person is right now.

1. **Choose Locate a Member Online from the Members
   menu.**
2. **Type the person's screen name in the dialog box, and
   click OK.**

   You see where they are—or you learn that they are
   not signed on right now.

Getting Help

Help comes in many forms on America Online. The first
place to turn is the Help system. On a Macintosh, Help sits
on the Apple menu; on Windows, Help is its own menu.
   Help covers topics such as

- Access Numbers
- America Online Departments
- Changing your Modem Strings
- Changing your Setup
- Connecting in Alaska, Canada, or Hawaii
- Download Manager
- Entering and Storing your Password
- Entering Stored Passwords
- Getting Help on America Online
- Help with Error Messages
- How to Be a Guest
- Local Access Numbers
- Mail
- Problems
- Travelers Changing Localities
- Using FlashSessions

- Using TCP/IP to Connect
- Welcome to America Online

You can see that these topics do not cover everything you may want to do. They're heavily focused on the needs of the person who's signing up for the first time and requires some general guidance.

Getting a Lot More Help from Member Services

When you're connected to America Online, you can take advantage of its fantastic Members Services department.

Members Services is free. Whenever you go there, AOL closes all other windows (for which you have been being charged, minute by minute). Basically, that's good. But if you've been chatting, or using a gateway to communicate with some other system such as the Internet, you lose the contents of those windows. So save first!

1. **Choose Member Services from the Members menu.**

   Or you can choose Keyword, and type Help.

2. **When you see the warning that all other windows are going to be closed or hidden, click OK.**

   On the left you see the kind of help you can get while connected to AOL: live technical support, a bulletin board with other members, a set of prepared answers to common questions, and a chance to email the staff.

   Remember that any online help is free—you aren't paying for the time you spend straightening out a problem.

   On the right, you see what kind of help you can get even when you are not connected: you can telephone the support folks, get them to send you a fax about a commonly asked question, dial into a separate bulletin board full of technical info, or get the details on any command on a menu.

   For billing info or questions about the security of your account, click the icons at the top of the window.

Figure 3.10 *Member Services Window*

Finding Out about Your Bill

No matter how carefully you read the fine print, you may
have questions about how you're being charged, or you
may need to tell AOL about a change of address, or switch
credit cards. In the Member Services department, you can
get answers to questions such as:

- Which areas cost me extra? (Almost none. You pay extra
  to have something faxed, you pay for any product you
  order, and if you use the *San Jose Mercury*'s database,
  you pay a surcharge. And, by the way, Help itself incurs
  no charge whatsoever.)

- If I was unexpectedly disconnected, can I get credit?
  (Yes, but you need to fill out a form to get the credit.)

- When do you post charges to my account? (Every month,
  on the day you first signed on—a unique anniversary!)

1. **Choose Members Services from the Members menu.**
   Or you can choose Keyword, and type Help.

7. Click Post, to put the message up for others to respond to.

8. Tomorrow or the next day come back and open any messages that begin Re:, followed by your subject.

Chatting with a Customer Service Rep, Live

From 9 A.M. to 2 A.M. eastern standard time weekdays and from 12 noon to 9 P.M. EST on weekends, you can enter an imaginary room where there's at least one Customer Service person to answer questions from you and other customers. When you first drop in, you can listen in, without asking a question, just to see what's going on. Then you can type your question, and see an answer appear right after your question, on the screen.

The dialog between you and the Customer Support person is going on now—real time. You aren't just posting a question, and waiting for someone to come in later and answer it; you are typing at the same time the customer support person is.

1. Choose Keyword from the Go To menu and type CSLive (for Customer Support Live), and click OK.

    You go to the Tech Live window, which warns you that AOL only offers customer support for its own software, and urges you to go to the Computing and Software department for help on another product.

2. Click Tech Live.

3. Double-click Tech Live Auditorium, in the list of topics.

    You get a notice urging you to find out what version you are using, before asking for help.

4. Click Tech Live.

    You get the rules for the Tech Live auditorium.

5. Click Tech Live again.

    You see the auditorium window.

6. **Click the Chat Rows icon, to pick a row to sit in, in this imaginary auditorium.**

7. **Choose a row.**

   If you are having trouble when connected, double-click a row from 1 to 10; if you can't connect, or if you have system problems, double-click a row from 11 to 19; and if you are having Internet woes, double-click row 20.

   This is a horrible interface, but I guess they are just trying to presort the questions. The idea is that you move to a row that has a Tech Help person sitting in it, and he or she helps you, or you get an answer from other folks in your row.

   You see a window with a lot of typing going on. Someone else is asking a question, or the Customer Service person is answering a question, and you are coming into the conversation in the middle. Take your time (Figure 3.12).

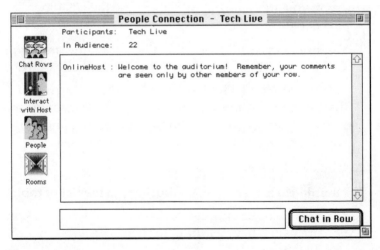

Figure 3.12   *Breaking into the conversation*

8. **Listen to the conversation, and when you see a real lull in the action, ask your question by typing in the**

box at the bottom of the window and clicking Chat in Row.

In a moment—or two, or three—you get a response. (You may have to wait while the customer service person answers someone else, but they are very swift.) I've found these folks very, very knowledgeable, and even when they aren't familiar with a problem, they go off, try stuff out, and come back in half a minute with suggestions. They get an A+ from me.

Writing a Note to Customer Support

For the moment, you can only do this on the Mac.

1. **Choose Member Services on the Members menu.**
2. **On the Member Services window, choose Email to the Staff, and in the windows that appears next, choose Email to the Staff again.**

   You see a window with a set of mailboxes (each devoted to a different subject).

3. **Click a mailbox, or the Suggestion Box.**

   You see a dialog box for you to write in, along with instructions.

4. **Write your question or complaint, and click Send.**

Making a Phone Call to Support

If all else fails, or if you can't get online to take advantage of all the support there, call the hotline. Right now, that's 1-800-827-6364. (As service expands, different numbers may be added, assigned to various groups of members.) Call between 3 P.M. and 11 P.M. EST.

Yes, you may have to wait awhile. That's the main reason I urge you to try other paths before turning to the phone.

You get one of those "Press One for X" call-processing systems, but you can always ask for a human. And when you get a human, you'll be pleasantly surprised, at least if your experience is like mine. One man spent 15 minutes walking me through the setup for my weirdo modem. He didn't just give one solution and hang up, the way a lot of these so-called customer support teams do. He made sure I signed on again, and succeeded, and even then he hung around to make sure he'd answered all my questions.

Jean Villanueva, VP of Corporate Communications, says that a lot of other companies measure their support team by the speed with which they get off the line. "We think it's more important to solve the problem in one call— it's much more productive to do that, even if it is a 25-minute call." It's certainly more satisfactory to us customers!

Interestingly, the bulk of the phone calls have to do with configuring a PC or a modem so the customer can make the first connection. The world is full of nonstandard modems, PCs with crazy cards in them, and little problems like a phone system that requires you to wait for 11 seconds between dialing 9 and dialing the rest of the outside number. The customer support folks walk you through these configuration and setup issues, sometimes literally letter by letter.

After people sign on, though, they get most of their information from the Help system, the Help buttons in dialog boxes, and the Member Services area.

Saving and Printing a Help Screen

You can save or print the information in any Help window.

1. **With the Help window open and active (it's on top), choose Save from the File menu, name the document, and tell AOL where to put the file.**

   AOL saves the text as an ASCII file (unformatted text only). You can open this file with any program that reads ASCII files.

2. **With the Help window open and active (it's on top), choose Print from the File menu, and then set the options in the dialog box as you wish.**

CHAPTER **4**

SENDING AND RECEIVING MAIL, MESSAGES, AND FILES

Electronic mail's a lot faster, and cheaper, than snail mail. The postal service, of course, will deliver a letter to anyone, even if they live on rural route 404 and don't have a computer. But if the person you're writing to has a computer, and if that computer's connected to a service such as America Online, AppleLink, CompuServe, Delphi, eWorld, GEnie, Internet, MCI Mail, or any of dozens of other private or public networks, you can write your message on the computer, send it electronically, and have it delivered a few moments later—without ever going near a printer, licking stamps, addressing an envelope, or going out to the mailbox.

While getting your message across quickly, AOL's e-mail lets you attach a file (as if you were slipping a floppy disk into the envelope with your letter), have the computer dispatch multiple copies, and automatically store a copy temporarily, in case you need to review it. All that happens in less than a second, electronically.

Downside: You can only use e-mail when sending to a
fellow computer user on some service somewhere; you
can't count on any formatting, such as boldface or special
fonts, getting through the system to the recipient; and you
can't tuck a dollar bill in for your nephew.

Preparing and Sending Mail

When I was a kid, I used to yearn for mail. I didn't get
many letters from relatives, so I started filling out the
coupons in the back of *National Geographic,* asking for all the
details on vacations in Canada, or Bolivia. Dealing with
mail on America Online reminds me of those big envelopes
stuffed with Chamber of Commerce letters and full-color
brochures. If you send out a lot of mail, you get a lot back.
In fact, you could get so much return mail that AOL sets a
limit on your mailbox. But there's no limit on the amount of
mail you can send out!

Composing Your Mail

You can compose a message anytime—whether you're
connected to America Online or not. In fact, lots of people
recommend writing offline, when you're not paying for
the time.

1. **Choose Compose Mail from the Mail menu.**

   You see a document, with room to fill in the recipient's
   address, state the subject, attach a particular file, ask
   for a return receipt, oh, and actually write in—AOL
   takes care of the return address, because it knows this
   mail is coming from you (Figure 4.1).

2. **Enter the recipient's e-mail address in the To box.**

   If the recipient is a member of America Online, you
   just type the person's screen name. If the person's
   using another service, you'll probably have to type a
   screen name, plus an *at* sign (@), followed by information such as their service, company, mainframe computer's name, and perhaps some suffix, such as .com

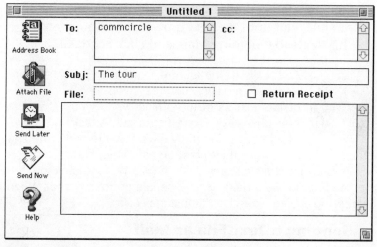

Figure 4.1   *Here's where you write your letter*

or .edu, identifying their organization as a commercial business or educational institution. You must get the exact screen name from the person you're writing to. On AOL the Members' Online Support folks can help you draft the rest of the address when sending through a gateway to another service. (The gateway's just a door from one service to another, but because the climate changes so dramatically, you can't assume anything will run as smoothly out there as it does inside AOL.)

3. **Add addresses for any people you want to send copies to, in the cc box.**

   To send a secret copy to a particular recipient, without revealing the fact to the others, put parentheses around that person's screen name (JonPrice).

4. **Write your letter in the big box at the bottom.**

5. **If you're online, click Send in Windows, or Send Now on the Mac.**

   If you're online, the message goes out right away. If you are not online, click Send Later. You can schedule a later FlashSession (in which the software signs on quickly, sends your mail, and signs off for you), or you can just wait until the next time you sign on; then choose Read Outgoing Mail, and click Send All.

 AOL calls it "netiquette," and it means there are rules of ordinary courtesy you should observe online, just as in the offline world (you know, the rest of reality). Don't flame out, attacking people. Most people feel they have to write and write and explode in order to get their point across when communicating online, because they lack any volume control, tone of voice, format, and so on. As a result, many people go to extremes when expressing any emotion. Don't. Just stay calm.

Sending a Text File as Mail

A text file is just letters and numbers, with a few marks of punctuation thrown in; it has no formatting, no special fonts, no art—just the ASCII codes, in a solid stream. On the Mac, you can grab any text file (created on your own word processor, or using the New command in AOL), slap an address on it, and send it as a letter to someone else. Such documents are not fully formatted letters, so AOL calls them memos.

1. **Open the text document using Open, or create the text file using New, on the File menu.**

2. **Choose Address Memo from the Mail menu.**

   Your text file appears as the message.

3. **Enter an address and subject, and send the mail.**

 You can also just copy material from a regular document and paste it right into your AOL mail, if you're willing to lose all your formatting. That's the way to send a text file in Windows.

Sending a File with Your Message

You have to write a message to accompany your file. Remember that AOL is not magic: **You** have to make sure that the recipient can read your file. Generally, that means you both have the same type of computer operating system (Macintosh, DOS, Windows), software that can read files from other operating systems, or software like Word that can read files created by Word on other operating systems.

1. Choose **Compose Mail**, and in the form, enter the address and subject, at a minimum.
2. Click **Attach File**, and in the file-handling dialog box, identify the file you want to send, and click **Add**.

   The filename appears in the File box.
3. Send your message.

   A copy of the file goes with it.

Checking on What You've Sent

Ooops! What did you say, exactly, in that mail you sent yesterday? AOL saves mail you sent in the last two weeks so you can review it, if you want.

1. Online, choose **Check Mail You've Sent from the Mail menu.**

   You see a list of mail you've sent out. You can copy your letter, or parts of it, if you want to send follow-up notices, or you can print it out. But you can't change the text. After all, it's already been delivered to the recipient. Use Show Status to see if it's been opened.

Sending a Letter via the U.S. Post Office

The office staff at AOL will be glad to take your message, print it out, and stuff it in an envelope, with a stamp on it—for a few dollars a letter. Your letter will be 70 characters wide; the first page will have 40 lines, and additional pages, up to a total of four pages, will contain 53 lines each.

To force a page break type >>> PAGE BREAK <<< on its own line. If you want the extra information normally supplied by e-mail (To, From, cc, Date, and Subject), you must supply that yourself, in your letter.

1. **Online, choose Fax/Paper Mail from the Mail menu.**

2. **Choose Send Fax/Paper Mail.**

3. **Enter the recipient's full name, up to 33 characters, as it would appear on an envelope, followed by @usmail.**

   For instance, Jonathan Price@usmail. If you want to send to several different people at postal addresses, separate them with commas, like this: Jonathan Price@usmail, Rooster Cogburn@usmail. Don't worry about addresses yet.

4. **Click Send in Windows, or Send Now on the Mac.**

   You're asked for the Return address to type on the envelope.

5. **Click ok.**

6. **Type the Return address, and then, when asked, the address of the recipient.**

   Nope, you can't send the same letter via U.S. mail and via AOL's e-mail at the same time; make copies, to do that.

Sending a Fax

You can have AOL send a message to someone's Group 3 fax machine anywhere in the U.S. or Canada (for a few dollars extra). Because this message remains electronic, you can send the same message to a mix of faxes and e-mail addresses.

Don't use any tab or control characters (they may come out as blots or tiny rectangles). Your text will be formatted for an 8.5-by-11-inch page, at 79 characters to the line, unless you put a Return earlier; 60 lines to the page, max. To force a page break, type >>> PAGE BREAK <<< on its own line.

Your fax will contain the To, cc, From (your screen name only), Date, and Subject lines you normally see on e-mail.

1. Online, choose Fax/Paper Mail from the Mail menu.
2. Choose Send Fax/Paper Mail.
3. Enter the recipient's full name, up to 20 characters, followed by the @ sign and area code and phone number.

   For instance, Jonathan Price@505 898-5407. If you want to send faxes to several different people, separate them with commas, like this: Jonathan Price@505 898-5407, Rooster Cogburn@800 800-8008.
4. Click Send in Windows, or Send Now on the Mac.
5. When told how much the fax will cost, confirm that you still really do want to send it.

Keeping Addresses in Your Address Book

Sometimes you remember a friend's name but not his or her screen name. Or you recall the screen name but can't decide whether it was AbeL7685 or AbeL8567. Your address book can help you track these details. In Windows, choose Edit Address Book from the Mail menu. Click Create, type the person's real name in the Group field and his or her screen name below. The Mac way is more complex:

1. On the Mac, choose Edit Address Book from the Mail menu (Figure 4.2).

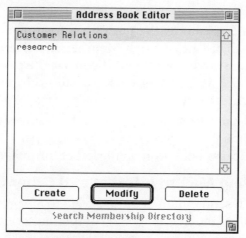

Figure 4.2   *The Address Book Editor on the Mac*

2. If you know the person's real name and screen name,
   click Create, and in the editing form (Figure 4.3), enter
   the person's real name at the top and the screen name
   in the Accounts section, then click ok.

Name: Customer Relations

Accounts: CS Manager

                    Cancel   OK

Figure 4.3   *The form in which you create new addresses and
modify old ones*

You can send out the same e-mail message to
everyone in a group this way. Just put the group
name in the first slot, and in the second, list everyone's screen name, separated by commas.

3. If you don't know the person's screen name, and you
   are online. Click Search Membership Directory, type
   in what you do know, and if you see the person on the
   list of possible names, click Add to Address Book and
   click Add Entry.

   The name or names appear in the Address Book. The
   next time you want to send mail to the person, just click
   the Address Book icon on the left of the mail dialog.

Sending Mail to Internet and Other Services

   You can send e-mail of up to 32K (6 to 8 pages long) to
people out on the Internet, or at competing services such
as CompuServe, for no extra cost. Here are just a few of

the places you can exchange mail with: CompuServe, AppleLink, AT&T Mail, MCI Mail, Prodigy, Delphi, and GEnie. You reach these services via the Internet.

These commercial services work pretty well, having been designed to have a friendly user interface. But the Internet cannot be said to have been designed; it more or less happened. Its origins lie in some of the most user-unfriendly areas of the country: the Pentagon and its associated think tanks at university and government labs around the country. But Internet soon sprawled beyond those hostile environments.

Now the Internet is a patchwork quilt stitched together by thousands of different grad students, hackers, government scientists, bureaucrats, professors, MIS departments, and corporations. So you can rarely be sure of anything, even death and taxes, on this network.

 Make sure you have the person's Internet address down exactly. You have to do this by phone, or word of mouth, or old-fashioned letter, because there is no such thing as a phone book for Internet. Nobody knows who's out there. For general advice about addressing the commercial services, choose Mail Gateway on the Mail menu, then click Internet Addresses, and open the article about the service.

And AOL won't even try to send any attached files because their chances for survival are low; they might get through, but then again, they might disintegrate somewhere in the process of moving from your computer through dozens or even hundreds of other computers, before reaching the other end of the line. Remember, Internet is what the phone system would have been like if the government hadn't granted a monopoly to AT&T—crude, flaky, brilliant, irritating, and inconsistent.

1. **Choose Compose Mail from the Mail menu.**
2. **In the To box, type the person's screen name (other-**

wise known as a user ID or username), followed by an @ sign, then the person's organization, and a suffix indicating what kind of organization that is (.edu for university, .com for business, and .gov for governmental agency).

Go all lowercase, and leave no spaces. For instance, if someone is at the University of New Mexico, you might write to dgill.unm.edu. Or if they are on CompuServe, you might write to: 12345.678@compuserve.com.

 If you need to tell people your Internet address, give them your screen name, followed by @aol.com. For instance, mine is jonprice@aol.com. Depending on the service they use, they may or may not need to add some extra stuff in front or in back; for example, a CompuServe user would have to address me as: >INTERNET:jonprice@aol.com.

Receiving Mail

Your mailbox can store more than 500 pieces of mail at any one time, from whatever source—Internet, Mars, or other members of AOL. If you get more mail than that, it's thrown away. If you are expecting a ton of mail, you must delete mail as fast as you read it, to make room for more.

 Once you've read a piece of mail, it stays in your mailbox for another week, then gets deleted automatically. If you haven't read it, it survives for only five weeks. To preserve a piece of mail, you must choose Save or Print from the File menu, while the letter's open in front of you, and place a copy on disk. You can also make mail new again, so it stays in your mailbox longer: while reading the mail, click Keep as New.

If you want a friend to send you mail from another commercial service, or directly through Internet, your basic

address is your screename followed by @aol.com. Mine is
Jonprice@aol.com. But some other services require additions at one end or another. To help your friend get the
address right, choose Mail Gateway from the Mail menu
then choose Receiving Mail from Other Services, and double-click the service.

Reading Your Mail Online

When you sign on, you'll be told whether or not you
have mail waiting for you. Look for the Mail icon.

1. **If the Icon says you have mail, click the icon to get a
   list of the messages, with the oldest mail at the top.
   Or if you have already been online awhile, choose
   Read New Mail from the Mail menu (Figure 4.4).**

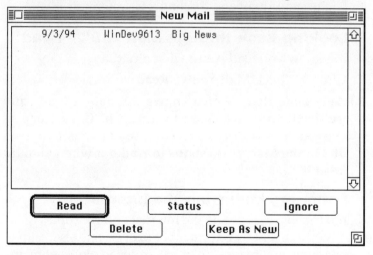

Figure 4.4   *The Mail window, with incoming mail*

If you know you never want to read the message, click
Ignore to have it removed later, or Delete to get rid of it
now. If you've read a piece of mail, but want to keep it
in the mailbox, click Keep as New.

2. **Double-click the subject to read the message.**
3. **You can now decide what to do with the mail.**

- If you want to **pass it along** to someone else, click Forward and enter the person's screen name.

- If you want to **respond** to the author, or to everyone who got a copy of the message, click Reply or Reply to All.

- To **save a copy** in your Online Mail folder, which is probably still in the same folder as your America Online software, click Save to Flashmail on the Mac. In Windows, use Save.

- To **print** a copy, choose Print from the File menu.

   (This is the same folder the software uses to store any mail gathered during one of the fast-in, fast-out connections called a FlashSession, where the software fetches your mail and disconnects, automatically.)

Looking Back through Mail You've Read

You know you read it, but what did it say?

1. Choose Check Mail You've Read.

2. Select the item (which shows the date, sender, and subject), and click Read to reread it. Click Keep as New to have an item treated as if you've not yet read it. On the Mac, click Status to find out when you did read it.

Soliciting Mail from the Internet

You can join a group on the Internet and get copies of every message sent by one member to everyone else; with some groups, you're looking at half-a-dozen pieces of mail every week, with others, 200 a day. So brace yourself. You've got to be interested in the subject, or the stream of incoming mail begins to look more like a flood. But, if you've got a hobby, a work specialty, or even just a lot of curiosity about a subject, here's how to find a mailing list and get on it.

1. Choose Keyword on the Go To menu and type Internet.

   The Internet Connection appears (Figure 4.5).

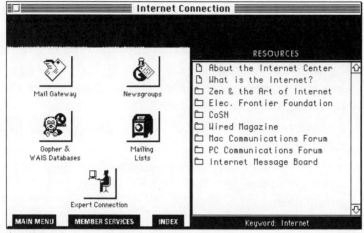

Figure 4.5 *Internet window*

2. In the Internet Connection window, click Mailing Lists.

You see a list of articles on the left, and the icon for searching for mailing lists on the right (Figure 4.6).

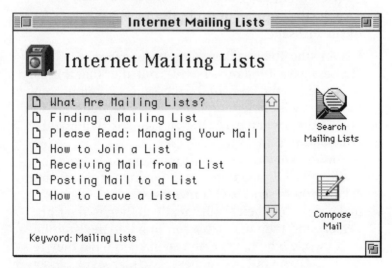

Figure 4.6 *Internet Mailing Lists*

3. **On the right of the Internet Mailing List window, click Search Mailing Lists.**

4. **At the top of the window that appears, type in a topic you're interested in.**

   In a few moments, you see the names of any mailing lists that deal with that subject.

5. **To find out a little more about any group on the list, double-click one.**

   You see a description of their purpose, members, and terms for admission. (You can't always just get in automatically.)

6. **Save, print, or copy the entire description of any mailing list you want to subscribe to.**

   Usually, you have to write to someone called .listserv (that is, the administrator of the list of members up on the server). You copy this info so you don't make a mistake later.

7. **Choose Compose Mail from the Mail menu.**

8. **Use the description to fill in the To, subject, and body of the message.**

   Usually the To box takes some awful expression like "listserv.gargantua.brown.edu," but after that things get easier. In the body of the message, all you usually have to say is something like "Subscribe," and give your ordinary name. (AOL takes care of giving your e-mail address.)

   You're likely to get a confirming message from the mailing list administrator, apologizing for asking, but asking you to send back a message such as OK, to make sure that their mail is really getting to the right person, and they're not just sending it to the Kremlin, or someone who has no interest at all in what they're getting. Then you'll get a message back, saying, essentially, "Got your OK. You're subscribed." From that second on, you start getting any messages that are being distributed to people on the mailing list.

 When you reply, make sure you are sending a message to the mailing list in general, not just to the person who posted a particular message. Read the TO box when you reply. (Of course, you may want to send a private comment directly to that person, in which case you might leave their e-mail address in the TO box.)

Sending and Receiving in a Flash

You can write messages offline during the day and then leave your computer on, telling it to send all that mail after the phone rates go down (usually at night), and at the same time pick up whatever mail has piled up in your mailbox and bring it all back to your hard disk for you to read later. That kind of whizbang session, known as a FlashSession, goes by itself; you set it up earlier, but the computer and the AOL software are in charge.

FlashSessions mean you save money, and you stay off the phone line when others might want to use it. You can also prepare a whole bunch of mail at once, go to bed, and leave it to the computer to send it all.

Remember: You can always get your mail the old-fashioned way, by signing on and asking to read your new mail. FlashSessions are just an extra convenience.

To Prepare for a Regular FlashSession

You might as well do this offline.

1. **Launch America Online, and choose FlashSessions from the Mail menu.**
   You see the FlashSession dialog box.

   You can specify what will occur during your flash sessions: you can retrieve incoming mail, send outgoing mail, and download any files you have previously selected for downloading. I recommend you click all three options.

2. In the box at the right of the FlashSession dialog box, choose what you want to send and receive—incoming files you stored earlier in the Download Manager, incoming mail, or outgoing mail.

    A check mark appears next to the ones you've chosen.

3. To make sure your computer can sign on by itself, click the icon of the lock and key, then enter the password to be used automatically during a FlashSession, and click OK.

4. Click Schedule FlashSession.

    You see the scheduler.

5. Edit the time you want to have the session, and specify how often you want the sessions (every half hour, once a day), then identify which days you want those sessions to take place. Click OK.

 Windows users can get a version of FlashSessions using software from outside AOL. Choose Keyword, type Filesearch, then type Whalex. But remember, AOL won't help you with this product, so don't download it if you feel insecure.

6. Close the FlashSession dialog.

7. Choose Download Manager from the File menu, and in the window, click Select Destination.

    You need to specify where the incoming material should be stored, when it arrives.

8. Select a directory or folder for your files, and click Save. Then close the Download Manager window.

9. Either keep the computer on, with America Online as the active application, or make America Online the startup application and use an electric timer to turn on the computer at the right time.

10. Later, if you want to see how a FlashSession went, choose View Results from the FlashSession dialog box.

You see a list of files successfully downloaded (Figure 4.7). You can also click Get Session Status in that window to find out whether all your mail went out OK and how long the session took.

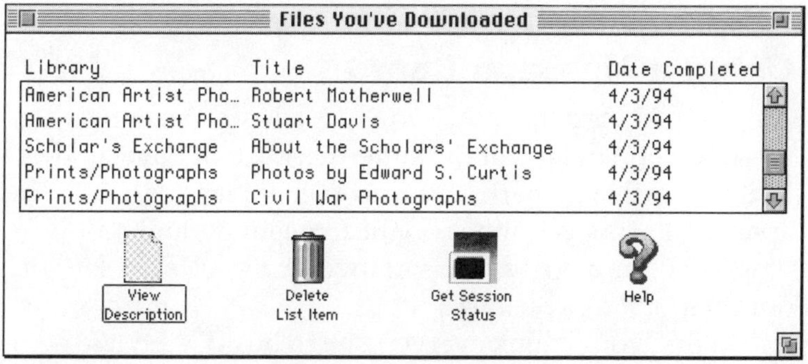

Figure 4.7   *List of files downloaded during FlashSessions*

To Read Mail That Arrived During a FlashSession

So all this mail comes in during the night, at your scheduled 3 A.M. session, and you wonder if any of it's crucial, so you decide to read through it.

1. **Before signing on, choose Read Incoming Mail from the Mail menu.**

   You see a list of the mail that's come in during that last FlashSession.

2. **Select any line (with the date, sender, and subject) and click Read.**

3. **If you wish, forward the mail or reply.**

   Your forwards or replies will go out the next time you have a FlashSession, or the next time you actually sign on, open the documents, and click Send Now.

Did you put together a big pile of outgoing mail, only to forget what you said to BillyBob? Not to worry. Use the Read Outgoing Mail command on the File menu on the Mac. In Windows, you can use Check Mail You've Sent after sending.

Using a Message Board

A message board, usually known as a *board*, resembles those bulletin boards at the supermarket that have landlords advertising apartments, people looking for apartments, notices about political meetings, and ads for work. Online, a board tends to involve more exchanges of opinions and less business.

At first you'll think everyone has a board. And it's almost true. When you look at all the boards on America Online, and then add all the other ones available through the Internet, you can understand why even the White House has set up a board. Want to get this year's budget package? A position paper on crime? Tell the president what you think about a hot issue? Just use the White House message board.

Finding a Message Board—And Getting the Message

Browse until you find a forum devoted to some subject you'd like to swap opinions about. In most message boards, you'll find a mix of rank amateurs—people who just wandered in to ask a question of the experts—and aficionados—people who are obsessed with the subject, know everything about it, and dial in every day to update their fellows.

Exchanging messages with other people who are as interested as you are in the subject can become a vital part of your routine, one you look forward to and rarely miss. To others, such interest borders on the obsessive. OK, you've been warned.

1. **Find a forum you're interested in, and look for an icon showing a pushpin holding down a note.**

    That's the icon for the message board or boards.

2. **Click the Message Board.**

    You see a window telling you how many categories of information you can find messages about; how many messages have been posted, all told; and the date of the latest posting. You can tell how popular the message board is, and how current.

3. **Click List Categories to find out how the messages have been organized.**

 If you keep coming back to the same forum's message boards, take advantage of two other buttons, Find New and Find Since, to ignore old messages and focus on the latest ones.

You see the major areas in which messages have been posted (Figure 4.8).

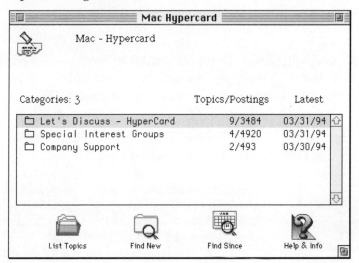

Figure 4.8   *A listing of the categories of messages in one forum's board*

4. **Select a category in the list, and click List Topics (Figure 4.9).**

   You're likely to see subcategories within the category.

```
▤░░  Let's Discuss - HyperCard  ░░▤

   ⬗     THE place for exchanging questions, answers and
  ▨▧     opinions on HyperCard. Find the latest news on
         HyperCard 2.0.


Categories: 9                    Topics/Postings    Latest
┌─────────────────────────────────────────────────────┐
│ 🗀 Forum Business/General Q & A      26/608   03/31/94 ⬆│
│ 🗀 HyperCard Beginner's Corner       27/653   03/31/94 ▨│
│ 🗀 Commercial & P.D. Stacks          17/151   03/26/94  │
│ 🗀 AppleScript                        5/92    03/15/94  │
│ 🗀 Programming & Scripting           40/688   03/31/94  │
│ 🗀 XCMD's & XFCN's                   22/252   03/31/94  │
│ 🗀 HyperCard 2.2 is here!            15/582   03/31/94 ⬇│
└─────────────────────────────────────────────────────┘

     🗂             🔍            📅            ❓
  List Topics    Find New     Find Since    Help & Info
```

Figure 4.9   *When you ask to see the topics inside a category, you may see subdirectories, or folders within folders*

5. **Keep clicking List Topics until you see icons offering to list the messages in a selected topic or let you read the first message in the topic area (Figure 4.10).**

   When you reach the lowest level of subdirectories or folders, you can select a topic and ask to see a list of messages, or read the first message in that topic.

 At this level in the hierarchy, you can usually click an icon called Create Topic to set up your own subdirectory or folder that will contain an exchange of messages on some hot subject you've just thought up. (If the icon's missing, you may not be allowed to create topic directories; that task has been reserved for the forum administrator.)

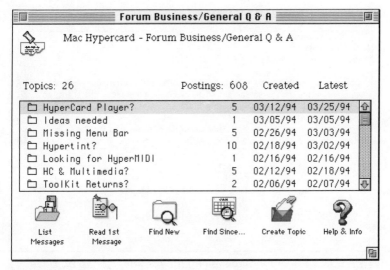

Figure 4.10 *Note List Messages and Read 1st Message icons*

6. Click Read 1st Message.

You see the actual text of a message (Figure 4.11).
Here's one in the White House board.

If you prefer to skim and dip, click List Messages, select an interesting subject, and then click Read Message.

Posting Your Own Messages for Everyone

Within a few minutes, you'll be itching to respond. One way you can do that is to *post* a message to everyone who visits the message board: Essentially, you are pinning your own note up on the board.

1. **Click Message Board, click List Categories, and then keep clicking List Topics until you see icons offering to list the messages in a selected topic or let you read the first message in the topic area.**

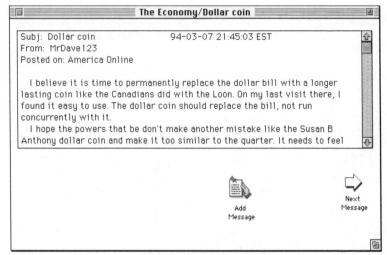

Figure 4.11 *A message telling the president what Mr. Dave 123 thinks of the idea of a new one-dollar coin*

Essentially, you have to go to the subdirectory or folder you're going to put your message into.

If you think that your topic constitutes an entirely new area, and you see an icon called Create Topics, click it and name your topic.

2. **Open a message, then click the icon called Add Message or Post Message.**

   You see a form in which you can write your message (Figure 4.12).

3. **Write your message, accepting the subject the system suggests or rewriting it, and then click Post.**

   If all is going well, the system responds with a dialog box that says your message has been added. Now everyone can read what you have to say.

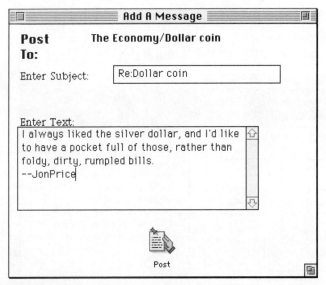

Figure 4.12   *Another concerned citizen voices his ideas about the dollar coin*

 To respond privately to one person who posted a message on an AOL message board, use Compose Mail from the Mail menu, and address it to the person's screen name. (On the other hand, when you are on Internet, you can click Reply and enter the person's address right there.)

Exploring a Newsgroup on Internet

Newsgroups started out as clusters of folks who were interested in the same subject. Now, thanks to the far-flung Internet, people from different institutions, backgrounds, and countries can get together to communicate. They raise questions, argue about answers, and offer each other advice.

No one knows why these groups are associated with news, because mostly they just provide a forum for discussion. But you'll hear them called USENET news, Net News, Internet News, and News. By whatever name, they resemble AOL's Message Boards.

1. **On the Go To Menu, choose Keyword and type Internet.**

   You go to the Internet Connection (Figure 4.13).

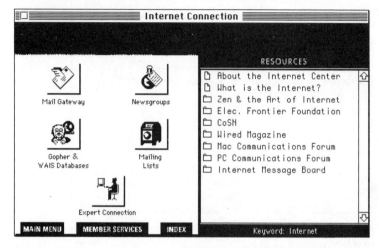

Figure 4.13 *The Internet connection, with the Newsgroups icon*

2. **Click the Newsgroups icon (Figure 4.14).**

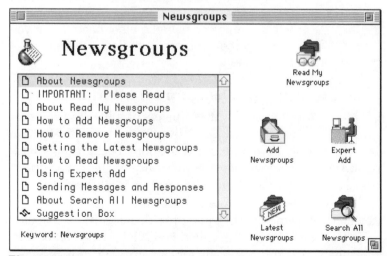

Figure 4.14 *The Newsgroups window*

3. **Click Read My Newsgroups to scan the list of Newsgroups that you have picked, or, if you're new, the list that AOL suggests as a starting point (Figure 4.15).**

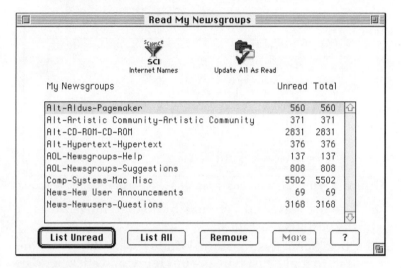

Figure 4.15 *The list of newsgroups in your Read My Newsgroups window*

 If you have recently been reading through this newsgroup, choose List Unread if you want to avoid rereading some messages.

4. **Select one of the newsgroups, and click List All or List All Subjects.**

    You see a list of the messages, or groups of messages, in that newsgroup (Figure 4.16). Check under Number to see how many messages relate to the topic.

5. **Click Read Messages to read the first in whatever set you select.**

    You see the start of an actual message, at last (Figure 4.17). This gibberish shows where the message came from and when.

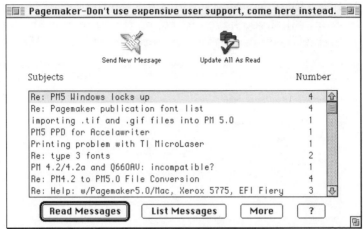

Figure 4.16 *Lists of messages, and groups of related messages*

6. Use the Next and Previous buttons to move through the various messages.

7. Click Send Response in Windows, or Reply on the Mac, to reply. Just type in your reply, and click Send or Send Now.

   AOL puts in the correct address for you.

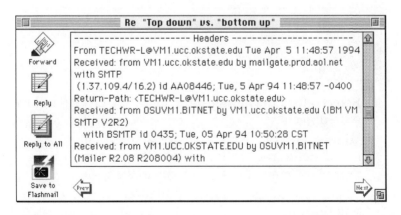

Figure 4.17 *The message has a lot of information at the top, showing where it came from, and when*

Going for Information on the Internet Using Gopher and WAIS

Gopher, an application created at the home of the Golden Gophers (University of Minnesota) helps you search through online phone books, library catalogs, newsgroups, and databases. If someone has put a Gopher-compliant (smile!) database online, you'll be able to browse through it to see if any records match your needs.

WAIS, the Wide-Area Information Server, was developed by Apple Computer, Dow Jones & Co., Thinking Machines, and KPMG Peat Marwick to store all kinds of material (but mostly text) in a way that ordinary folks will find easy to use. The companies have made WAIS a standard, so anyone can put their information into this form on a WAIS server (serving you with information) and as a client you can look it up. You just type what you want to find out about, and WAIS looks through millions of documents to see if the actual text contains those words, close together. You pose your question to a collection of *servers* (gigantic hard disks with tons of information on each one), narrow down your choices to a few servers that seem to have relevant info, and then query them.

1. **Choose Keyword from the Go To menu and enter Internet.**
2. **On the Internet Connection window, click Gopher and WAIS databases.**

   You see the Gopher and WAIS window (Figure 4.18).
3. **Double-click on a category to see its contents (Figure 4.19).**
4. **Keep double-clicking to open subdirectory after subdirectory until you finally reach a set of files. Double-click one of those files to read it, if it is text, or to download it if it happens to be an image file.**

   You can preserve any text by choosing Save or Print from the File menu.

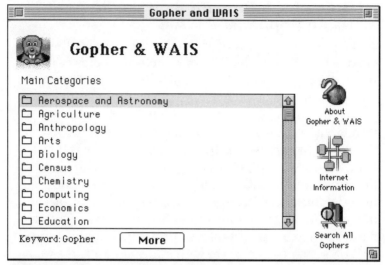

Figure 4.18 *The window devoted to go-fer-it searching, and wide-area information searching*

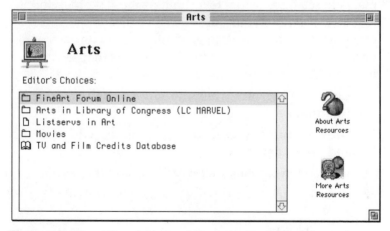

Figure 4.19 *The contents of the Arts subdirectory*

Downloading and Uploading Files

America Online more than pays you back for your monthly investment if you take advantage of its many libraries of software in every category, plus sample files of every type and taste. You can download these files from their mainframe computers to yours, bringing them down so that you can use them. If you have something to share with the world, you can upload files from your computer to the mainframe, making your own work available to anyone who happens on it.

For any online library, there's a librarian—someone who monitors every file that comes in, runs a virus check on it, and decides whether or not to post it, that is, make it visible to people who come browsing through the lists of files. Not an easy job. On an average day, in some libraries, the person in charge must review a dozen applications, and a dozen new files, just to keep up.

Your America Online software includes a module called the Download Manager; this manager acts like a traffic cop, making sure that all your files get in queue, and when summoned, come down the right phone lines to you.

Specifying Where to Put Downloaded Files—Beforehand

You use the Download Manager to tell America Online where to put any files that it downloads to you. Generally, you'll find it easier to collect them all in one location, and then, when you've quit America Online altogether, to move the files to their best locations.

1. **Choose Download Manager from the File menu.**

   You see a window displaying whatever files you have recently chosen to download, if they have not been downloaded (Figure 4.20).

2. **Click Select Destination, at the bottom.**

3. **Specify a directory (a folder, not a file). Double click to find the subdirectory, then click ok to select it.**

Finding the Right File and Downloading It

Finding the right file can be dizzying at first, because there are so many files ready to be downloaded. But basically, any time you get a list of documents, applications, or

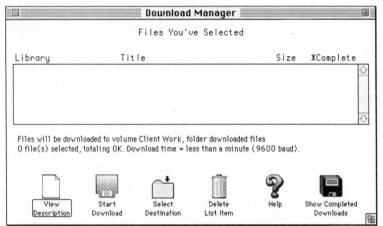

Figure 4.20 *The Download Manager, empty*

whatever, you get a set of buttons that look like the ones
shown in Figure 4.21. These buttons let you show more
files, download the selected one now, or hand it off to the
Download Manager for downloading later.

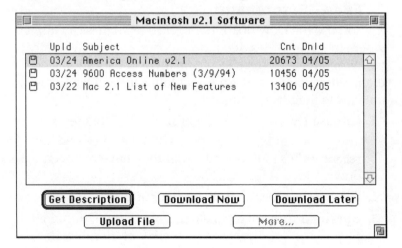

Figure 4.21 *Buttons letting you download now or later*

- **To see more files, click More.**

  More is the most overlooked button in America Online. The system usually only shows you the first 10 or 20 files, because that number can be sent quickly, and you may discover that nothing in the area interests you. But if you are interested, remember to look for a little note that says something like, "1-10 of 160 files," and the More button is active. You do not lose the names of files you have already seen; the new files simply fill in at the end of the list.

- **If you want to find out how big a selected file is, how long it will take to download, or what it consists of, click Get Description.**

  Once you've selected a file you want to download, you can have it sent to you right away, or you can put it into a list of downloads and wait until the end of the session, or even a later FlashSession (on the Mac), to have all of them downloaded.

- **If you are so eager to see the file that you are willing to twiddle your thumbs for a few minutes, right now, click Download Now.**

- **If you can wait, click Download Later.**

  Download Later adds the file to the list of files the Download Manager maintains, waiting for the opportunity to send them to you all at once, in a Flash-Session. That might take place at the end of your online session, just before you sign off, or later tonight, when you have your computer dial in for you.

- **If you want to download at the end of your online session, choose Download Manager from the File menu.**

  You see the Download Manager window. The buttons let you view a description of any file (the same description you read earlier when you picked the file in the first place), start downloading, change the destination of downloads, delete an item from the list, or show you what's already been downloaded in case you forgot. These buttons give you a lot of information, but don't overlook the summary above them, telling you how long the total downloading will take. You have to decide whether you can afford to tie up your computer that long or not.

- **If you don't want to download now, sign off but set up a FlashSession for a better time.**

All files that are downloaded are saved in whatever directory you specified as the destination (when you were using the Download Manager), and, if any of those files came in compressed form—shrunk in order to take less time zipping down the phone line—America Online decompresses them for you, if it can.

 You may find two files with similar names next to each other; the one that ends in something like .sit, .ZIP, .ARC, or .exe is likely to be a compacted file created as a StuffIt, PKZip, AOL archive, or self-extracting file. Test out the other file. If that's in good shape, you can toss the compressed version away.

Deciding What to Upload

Consider whether or not other people will find your file useful. Have you gotten all the bugs out? Would another person who's interested in the same subject have any questions? Fix the file up before you go public.

And make sure you own what you're going to send. You wrote it, you created it, you didn't make this file as an employee of some big company. You didn't just scan someone else's picture.

Here's what one manager says: "Do not upload copyrighted files unless you are the copyright holder, or have, and can present written permission from the copyright holder to the forum leader. Simple rule: if it is scanned, do not upload it unless you have written permission from the copyright holder." He then repeats this caution in an attached file, and in three other guidelines. Please take him seriously.

If you decide you can't resist stealing other people's work, you'll find plenty of folks who are glad to accept your pirated material down at your local user group.

Compressing a File to Upload

When you're considering putting one of your documents, or some software you've created, up in a forum for other folks to download, you need to make that process of downloading go as quickly as possible. You need to compress your file, shrinking its size without losing its details—using a utility that the other folks are likely to have. On the Macintosh, use StuffIt, or StuffIt Deluxe, and take advantage of America Online's ability to "unstuff" at the other end; for Windows, use a compression utility such as PKZIP. (You can find a copy online; choose Search Software Libraries from the Go To menu and type zip to find some variation.)

Compress the file beforehand. And make sure that when you get around to uploading, you are sending the compressed version. It'll take half as long for other people to download, and that's a big incentive to try your file out.

Uploading

First, visit the forum you intend to grace with your uploads. If the forum has several libraries, look in each one; check out their contents; decide which subdirectory is most appropriate for your material.

1. **Click Upload File, or click a button named Upload a File.**

   You see the Upload File Information window, in which you describe your file (Figure 4.22).

2. **Give your file an interesting and accurate name.**

   Often, the subject is what helps a person decide whether or not to download.

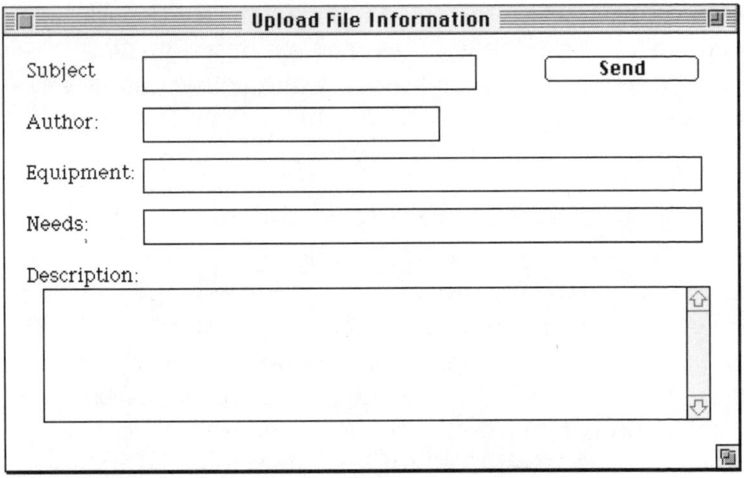

Figure 4.22   *You need to describe your file for others*

3. Identify yourself, somehow, as the author.
4. Be clear about what computer you need to run the application or open the file.
5. Spell out what application or type of application the user needs to read your file.
6. Give an exciting plug for your file, without going gaga.

   What makes your file unusual, exciting, helpful? Think about the file from their point of view. What makes it worth spending their time on?

7. **In Windows, click Send.**

   Your file goes on up the line. When it arrives, the America Online staff will check it for viruses (tiny applications that eat holes in your other applications, files, or hard disks); correct any mistakes you've made in referring to keywords, program names, and so on; and then, as long as the file seems unobjectionable, post it for others to download.

   And get this: You get a credit for any time you spend uploading!

CHAPTER **5**

Participating in Games, Game Shows, and Other Auditorium Events

A lot of people just play games online. Through the network, they find partners, opponents, and fellow aficionados who love to talk about the games. You can indulge in individual chats about video games, try out investment simulations, do role-playing, play strategy games, or try your luck in a trivia forum. Most games appear in the Entertainment department, but you may find game-playing going on almost anywhere.

For instance, one of the biggest rooms in America Online, the Center Stage, hosts a series of game shows in which you and several hundred other members compete in electronic versions of anagrams, tic-tac-toe, and make-a-word.

That auditorium is also used for mass events such as introducing VIPs to members, who get to ask questions and make comments. You can interact with the guest, electronically. (Another auditorium, the Rotunda, is devoted to computer topics.)

Playing Games

I'm not going to get into the detailed rules. You can find those online. But I'm going to give you an idea of what it's like to play games online. It's a lot weirder than anything you ever tried with Monopoly.

There are more people involved. You don't know them, so you can't predict what they will say or do.

Going to the Online Gaming Forums

Deep in the Entertainment department, this forum draws together players, designers, and vendors of all kinds of computer games.

1. **Choose Keyword from the Go To menu, and type gaming.**

   You enter the Online Gaming Forums (Figure 5.1).

Figure 5.1   *The Online Gaming Forums*

2. **To exchange tips, request information, or join a club, choose the General Information Board and browse the directories.**

   You can, for instance, join clubs devoted to Mortal Kombat, NBA Jam, Lemmings, and X-Wing.

Free-Form Games

Take on a character and interact with other folks who are paladins, swashbucklers, and dream weavers. The forum provides the environment, and you bring the character.

 Because these games take place electronically, without pictures and without a board, you must go through elaborate setups—just to fight another paladin, you need to go through such a complex drill that you may think you are doing programming. Even counting points requires applying half-a-dozen formulas.

1. **Choose Keyword from the Go To menu and type RDI (short for Red Dragon Inn).**

   You see the Free-Form Gaming Forum (Figure 5.2).

```
▤▢▭▬▬  FREE-FORM GAMING FORUM  ▬▬▬
  ▯ Welcome to the FFGF - Please Read
  ▯ FFGF Forum News                 8/1/94
  ▱ Message Board Center
  ▭ The Arena
  ▨ Red Dragon's Great Hall
  ▤ Free-Form Gaming Forum Library
  ▯ Duel of Swords Standings 9/1/94
  ▯ Duel of Fists Standings 8/19/94
  ▭ More...

                    ┌──────────────┐
                    │    Open      │
                    └──────────────┘
```

Figure 5.2   *The Free-Form Gaming Forum*

Click the icon that looks like a piece of paper with the corner turned down, for a document; click the curlicue on its side and the pushpin for message boards; and click the two people face to face for chats.

2. **Open the Arena directory, and read the rules.**

3. **Choose a character type from the Character Classes folders (Cleric, Cleric-Magic User, Cleric-Thief, Druid, Druid-Illusionist, and so on), and save the information about that class.**

4. **Within your class limitations, pick a hand-to-hand weapon and missile.**

5. **Send e-mail describing your character class and weapon choices to OGF Roane (or the current ref), who will figure out hit points, spell points, and rank points.**

6. **Find a character to do a battle with, and work with Arena officials to set up a match during regular Arena hours, between 8 P.M. and 11 P.M. eastern standard time, Wednesday through Sunday.**

7. **Report to the Arena, and put up your money (Guild Points). Meet your official, who will direct the combat.**

8. **To make a move, cast a spell, make an attack, or defend yourself, send an Instant Message to the official.**

These moves must follow a standard syntax, explained in the Arena Rules. If a spell fizzles, you lose points.

You know you're the winner at the end if your character is still standing. If you win, you get healed, your spells get refueled, and you get bonus hit points or spell points. The loser loses points and can't play again that day.

Down at the trading post, you can buy scrolls ("a tad unreliable," the ad says), spells, stones, enchantments, and potions. Unfortunately for those of us who like runes and rhymes, you don't really get a poetic spell—you just pay for its effect.

For ongoing stories to which you can contribute or ask about, turn to Dragon Tales or some of the other boards. You'll find fake medieval trappings on stories revolving around people's dreams of grotesque power, psychic abilities, charms, and so on (mostly written, as far as I can tell, by people lacking any real magic). The creators seem to put more energy into fantasy than into developing the craft they long for.

To Jump into Other Role-Playing Games

From the first one, Dungeons and Dragons, to GURPS, the all-purpose Generic Universal Role-Playing System, you can play variations online, gossip about the offline versions, and play for hours.

1. **Choose Keyword from the Go To menu, type Gaming directory, and then open the Role-Playing Games directory.**

2. **Check out the Game Schedules, find one you think might be interesting, whether it takes place live, by e-mail, or on a bulletin board with messages. See if the Game Moderator will accept someone of your level of skill.**

3. **Write the Game Moderator, and ask for help in creating a character.**

 Another route takes you to the General Messaging board within the Role-Playing Forum, where Game Moderators put up notices asking for players to join them in a campaign.

To Play Games "By Mail"

Taking off from the chess-by-postcard phenomenon, these games include board games, fantasies, historical or military strategy, and science fiction. The games may last

for months. You dial in, make your move via e-mail or a
bulletin board, and exit. Don't worry about committing a
whole evening to it.

A game master runs the show. He or she opens the
topic in a bulletin board, and you write in to join. The rules
may not be the same as you used in the board game version, so read those rules early!

- **Choose Keyword from the Go To menu, type Gaming,
  and then open the Play-By-Mail and Strategy Gaming
  directory (Figure 5.3).**

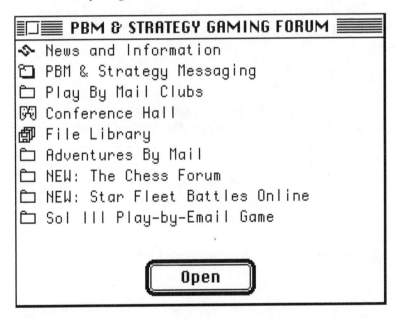

Figure 5.3   *Games you can play by e-mail or snail mail*

To Find Out about New Games

1. Choose Keyword from the Go To menu, and type
   Gaming.
2. In the Online Gaming Forums window, click the icon
   called GameBase (Figure 5.4).

Figure 5.4 *The GameBase is a database of information about games, game vendors, and the development of new games*

3. Open the Reviews folder, and look up the game.

These reviews are hard-hitting. No PR fluff here.

In the Online Gaming Forums window, also check out the Conference Schedule for interviews with developers you like, and browse the Game Designers Forum.

Bulls and Bears

When you join this online game, you get an imaginary $100,000 line of game credit to place orders for stocks and options. You can then trade these until the end of the month. The top ten players are posted on the menu.

This game has generated dozens of complaints because although you get current quotes to work with (this itself is a technological marvel), all your buys and sells are recorded at the last price of the day. Also, the ideal participant is going for his or her broker's license, according to the online gossip. If you don't know anything about the market, don't bother with this. Oh, and just to challenge you even more, the interface is that of an ancient mainframe: character-based, with secret codes, and you have to remember the right number for every command or you get snapped at ("INVALID SELECTION!"). Or, if you're lucky, you may be able to scroll backward to find the code you need (Figure 5.5). Still up for the challenge? Read on.

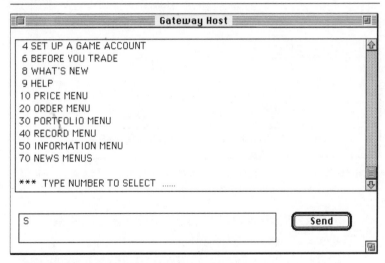

Figure 5.5 *The opening list of codes for Bulls and Bears*

1. On the Entertainment Department list, choose Bulls and Bears, then choose Enter Bulls and Bears/E*TRADE.

2. Type 4 to Set Up a Game Account, and press Send. When asked, give your handle, or the name you want to go by, in the game.

3. Type S to sign up, then give your handle, or the name you want to go by.

4. Choose Stocks and Options (option 1) or Stocks Only (option 2). If asked, give your handle.

5. Type 20 to see the Order Menu, type 21 to Buy Stocks, type 211 to Buy or Sell Stocks, and identify the portfolio you want to modify (if you set up more than one).

   You can have several portfolios.

6. Type in the stock symbol, and choose Buy by typing B or Sell by typing S (Figure 5.6).

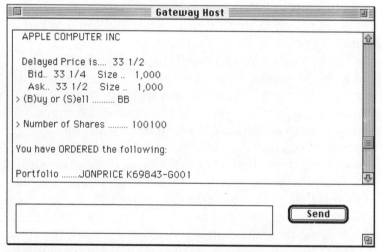

```
═╤════════════════ Gateway Host ════════════════╤═

  APPLE COMPUTER INC                                ⇧

  Delayed Price is.... 33 1/2
   Bid.. 33 1/4   Size ..  1,000
   Ask.. 33 1/2   Size ..  1,000
  > (B)uy or (S)ell ......... BB

  > Number of Shares ......... 100100

  You have ORDERED the following:

  Portfolio ........JONPRICE K69843-G001          ⇩

  ┌─────────────────────────────┐  ┌──────────┐
  │                             │  │   Send   │
  └─────────────────────────────┘  └──────────┘
```

Figure 5.6 *I have just bought 100 shares. (Due to a bug, the order of 100 has been duplicated as 100100; this kind of error is common in Bulls and Bears.)*

If you need to look up a company symbol, look in Menu 52.

7. Specify the number of shares you want to purchase. Confirm that you understand this is a game order only, and that it is correct, by typing Y.

8. To buy Options, type 221, click Send, then enter the company symbol, and specify the number of Options you want to buy.

Remember: This is only a game. Your purchases here have no effect on your regular account, if you maintain one online.

9. **To quit, type 0 (that's a zero) and click Send.**

Attending a Game Show, a Center Stage, or a Rotunda Event

You can go to the America Online equivalent of Radio City Music Hall or the *Jeopardy* TV studio to participate in game shows, lectures by VIPs, and other large public events. These take place in auditoriums such as the Rotunda and Center Stage.

The Rotunda sponsors events focused on computing and software. Center Stage events bring together hundreds of people for a game show or a lecture from someone famous with questions afterward. In these auditoriums, you sit in rows of between four and eight seats, and you can hear what other people in your row are whispering, or asking the lecturer, if you want—or you can tune that stuff out. The folks onstage accept certain questions and respond to them, talking to everyone in the audience.

The game shows aren't too hard. In one, the host casts dice to come up with seven letters of the alphabet. Your job is to put them together into the longest word you can think of: The longer it is, the more points you get.

Locating the Calendar and Rules

Any event that's coming up in the Rotunda (the big auditorium mostly devoted to computer-related interviews with famous engineers and marketers) will probably be promoted on your sign-off screen; when the event's taking place, you'll see it on your sign-on screen. Similarly, you'll see some notices for game shows and events in the biggest auditorium of all, Center Stage.

1. **Choose Keyword from the Go To menu, and enter Rotunda or Center Stage.**

You can get to the Rotunda from the Computing Department window by choosing the special attractions tonight, then going into the Rotunda auditorium. You can reach Center Stage from any room in the People Connection by clicking the icon on the left.

2. **In the Center Stage area, open the Box Office directory to get a list of events. For the rules on game shows, click Game Show Rules.**

Here are a few of the bigtime games:

- 3-in-a-row: an electronic version of tic-tac-toe, played against computerized dice.

- Brainstorm: a variation on anagrams, in which you reassemble seven letters to make a new word.

- Grids: starting with four lines of four letters each, make words using letters that touch each other.

- Madscramble: a lot of letters you have to rearrange into a familiar phrase (SAYMOSEYEGOACE becomes "Easy Come Easy Go").

- Madvertising: guess whose slogan that was.

3. **In the Rotunda, open Upcoming Rotunda Events.**

In each area, you can get transcripts of some of the events that have been put on in the past. These archives give you what was said, in an ASCII text file, so you can seize quotes and use them in a word processing document.

Getting to the Game Show or Event the Fast Way

You can amble up to the events, clicking your way from department to forum and so on. Or you can go direct.

1. **Choose Keyword from the Go To menu, and enter Rotunda or Center Stage.**

You're assigned a row number and welcomed as a participant. Being a participant means you are a member of the audience, and can, if you wish, ask questions, make comments, or offer answers.

2. **To find out what row you are in, or to change rows, click Chat Rows. To talk with someone in your row, type a message and click the Chat in Row button on the bottom right (Figure 5.7).**

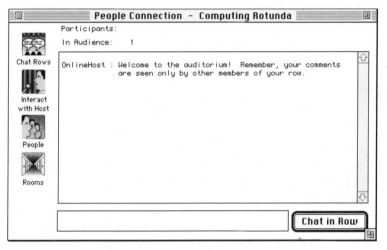

Figure 5.7 *The Chat Rows button in the top left lets you switch rows, if you need to*

3. **To participate in the event, click Interact with Host, type something in, and click Question, Comment, Vote, or Bid.**

Asking Questions and Making Comments

Your questions and comments pour into the host of your event or game show in the order received. The host ignores most of these, picks the best, and they are answered for the whole audience. In game shows, you may even win a prize if you guess the right answer (or question)—free time on AOL, software, hardware, or other merchandise.

1. **Click Interact With Host on the left in the dialog box; then click Send Question if the mike is turned on for your row, and type your question (Figure 5.8).**

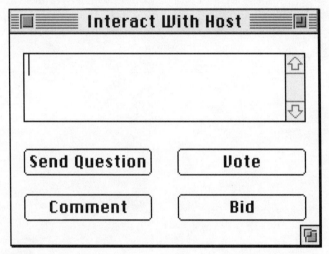

Figure 5.8 *The Interact With Host dialog box allows you to type something in, and then send it as a question, comment, vote, or bid.*

You see your question, preceded by your row number, onscreen; other people in your row see it, but the rest of the audience does not. The host, up onstage, receives many questions, discards some, and decides to answer others; do not ask the same question twice, just because it hasn't been answered yet—that just clogs up the system.

In Game Shows, you often use this feature to make a guess about the answer, too. You have about 30 seconds to get your answer in.

2. **Click Interact With Host, and in the dialog box, click Comment, if the mike is turned on for your row.**

In Game Shows, you can ask questions if the mike's on in your row, but no one listens to comments. If the mike's not on, the dialog box does not appear—you have to wait.

 In some events, you can bid on items offered for sale, using the Bid button in the Interact With Host dialog box. In other events, you can register your vote with the Vote button.

CHAPTER **6**

LEARNING ONLINE

With America Online, you can look up an odd assortment of facts, encyclopedia articles, magazine pieces, and statistics. You can learn a lot about education. You can take courses. You can even get help with your homework.

AOL, however, is not a library of books put online. In fact, only a tiny, tiny fraction of the books that you see in a public library are available online. The copyright holders don't want to let go of the text without a fee; and for works that are in the public domain, few people are willing to type them out and post them for free. You can look books up in libraries around the world, then, but you can't get the full texts online; for those, you have to go the old route of borrowing a book, or requesting one via interlibrary loan.

On America Online, you learn more from exchanging messages and mail with other people who are interested in what you are interested in. You get current tips about contemporary problems, rather than classics by John Dewey or Cardinal Newman.

Looking Up Information

The information you can look up on America Online is free. For that reason, you won't find the latest newsletters, inside dope, or full text of financial advisories. Those facts, whose value depends on getting them faster than your competitors can, can cost several thousand dollars an hour on other networks. AOL doesn't cater to businesses that way, so you'll need to go to the Dow Jones News Retrieval Service, Mead Data's Nexus, or Dialog to pry open those sophisticated databases.

What you can find, though, is amazing. America Online has persuaded many public institutions to provide some of their expertise; major magazines link you to their educational services, indexes, and some of their articles; and there's a whole encyclopedia. Plus—and this is AOL's strong point—you get to talk directly with other folks who are interested in the same subjects you are, and you can get valuable advice from them.

Using *Compton's Encyclopedia*

Here's a lot of information tailored for students: more than 8 million words, more than 5,000 articles, with 26,000 capsule articles, and an index with 63,503 entries. Alas, no pictures online yet.

1. **Choose Keyword from the Go To menu and type Reference.**

   You go to the Reference Desk (Figure 6.1).

2. **On the left click the icon for Compton's Encyclopedia.**

3. **On the right, click Search by Title.**

   You could choose to search through the full text of the encyclopedia, to see if your word shows up anywhere, but that takes a long time. Search titles first; then, if you don't find an article you can use, go to the full search. Either way, you get a form in which you can type (Figure 6.2).

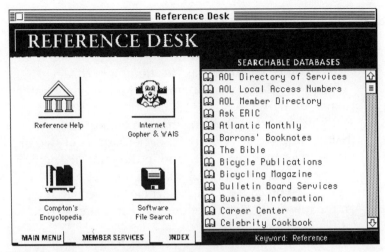

Figure 6.1 *The Reference Desk window*

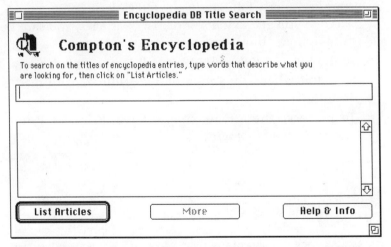

Figure 6.2 *Type the topic you want to look up, then click List Articles. The list of articles appears in the bottom box*

4. In the form, type the topic you're interested in, and click List Articles.

You should steer between topics that are so vague they might include most of the encyclopedia ("the universe") or so specific that they exclude almost everything ("General Lee when he was vacationing in 1870").

Don't use slang or nicknames. Try a last name, rather than a full name.

If your first try yields too many matches (articles that include the topic you mentioned), think of two or more topics that must be found in the same article: poetry and Baudelaire. Put an AND between the two topics. Or you can say, "If the article happens to touch on the following topic, exclude it." For instance: ducks NOT geese.

If your first try yields too few matches, expand your search by adding other topics, joined by OR, so if an article contains any of the topics, it will be added to your list: poetry OR Baudelaire OR Coleridge.

When you get an interesting list of articles, you can print it, if you think you might want to consult it again.

5. **In the list of articles, double-click to open a subdirectory, and when you spot an article you want to read, double-click to open it.**

6. **To preserve the article, choose Save, Print, or Print Text from the File menu.**

 If you want to save bits and pieces from several articles, choose New from the File menu, select the passages, choose Copy from the Edit menu, go to the document you created with New, and choose Paste from the Edit menu. You can collect all the passages in one document that way. Later, from inside your word processor, you can open that file and quote the material as coming from *Compton's Encyclopedia*.

If you quote from the encyclopedia, be sure to give it credit, like this: *Compton's Encyclopedia, Online Edition,* Downloaded from America Online, [date of downloading].

Using the Library of Congress

This library has reached the status of legend. Most people believe that anything that's ever been copyrighted in this country exists here, in two copies. Evidently, that's only sort-of true. But the collection is big. At best count, it has 97 million "books" (pamphlets, booklets, videotapes, so on). Unfortunately, you can't get at the electronic card catalog through this forum. And—they want you to know this!—it does not offer an online reference service. (To see what card catalogs are available online now, choose Keyword from the Go To menu, type Gopher, and open the Library Science section to search various libraries' catalogs, such as that of the University of California.)

1. **Choose Keyword from the Go To menu, and type Education.**

2. **Click the icon for the Library of Congress, on the left.**

   You see the Library of Congress Online window (Figure 6.3).

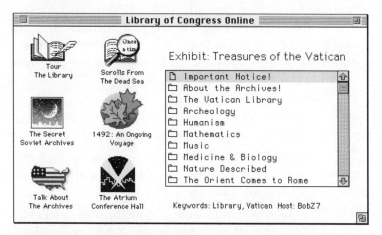

Figure 6.3   *The Library of Congress window changes as the exhibits come and go*

This forum gives you a picture of many Library of Congress current activities and shows:

- The American Memory Project is attempting to put a wide range of American photographs, film, video, sound, and text onto CD-ROM disks that could then be available at local libraries, or over America Online.

- The National Demonstration Lab is an experimental program trying out various interactive technologies for storing and delivering the nation's archives.

- The Center for the Book urges people to learn to read. It sponsors a board called Talk About Books, which attracts trivia buffs, and adults who seem to be learning to type.

- The National Library Service for the Blind and Physically Handicapped loans braille and recorded books, magazines, music scores, and large-print editions.

- The American Folklife Center preserves recordings of folk songs and tales. It has 40,000 hours of sound recording, 600,000 pages of manuscript, 200,000 ephemeral items, and 170,000 still photographs. But you can't download any of them yet. You can get a list of the center's free and for-sale publications and an overview of the collection. You can also chat about quilts, Jelly Roll Morton, and round barns on Talk About Folklife.

- The Copyright Office offers basic information, including how to search for copyright status, what needs to be copyrighted, and a message board about copyright law.

- The Dead Sea Scrolls exhibit. You can poke around the ruins or the caves, getting descriptions of the objects found, and, if you want, photographs.

  Take the tour to see what else is available. You can also get a Library Research Guide for special subjects (they answer commonly asked questions).

Exploring the Smithsonian

In the Education window, the Smithsonian appears as an icon on the left. Click that icon to open the Smithsonian window.

Figure 6.4 *The Smithsonian window*

You can get descriptions, catalogs, tour guides, and photos of objects in the attic of the nation—the Smithsonian includes the Air and Space Museum, the Hirshhorn Museum of Sculpture, the formal gowns of every First Lady, and reconstructions of dozens of rooms from the first pueblos to the latest space station.

- To find photographs you can download, click Smithsonian Photos. Fantastic! You can get first-rate professional photos from every period for personal use (unfortunately, most are not available for reproduction in publications). For an index of the art reproductions available, go to the National Museum of American Art, and open the Index—a lot easier than guessing what's in a picture based on its title alone.

- Magazines on space, art, natural history, and education appear in Smithsonian Publications.

- Preview exhibits, get descriptions of the permanent collections, join the Smithsonian associates.
- Ask the Smithsonian a question (click Smithsonian Information).
- Join Art Talk or Art Lovers' Exchange to gossip about art, trade tips on new exhibitions, and argue about whether or not the government ought to subsidize artists.

Browsing the National Geographic

In the Education department, these forums are set up for kids to explore. Just like the rows of yellow magazines in the library, these collections offer the raw material for reports on everything from ancient cities to zoos. Choose Keyword from the Go To menu, and type Geographic.

- To get the schedule of *National Geographic* TV specials, and supplements for classes, click Geographic TV.
- For the complete text of some recent articles, explore the scrolling list on the left.
- To get a list of previous articles on subjects such as acid rain, native American crafts, or the rain forest, choose Ask Geographic, and look in the Geographic Information Files (Figure 6.5). You can also post questions to be answered by *Geographic* staffers. (They asterisk (*) the queries they respond to, and you have to use a special button to see the responses.)
- To get educational materials, courses, supplementary video disks, CD-ROMs, and offprints, click the Geographic Education Program.

Scholastic Extra

Remember those pulp magazines that used to show up in school? Well, now they're online, complete with curriculum projects, tons of extras you can buy, and interviews with authors. You can use a sampling of the activities for about ten hours free, but you have to pay extra to get full use of the forum. Keyword: Scholastic.

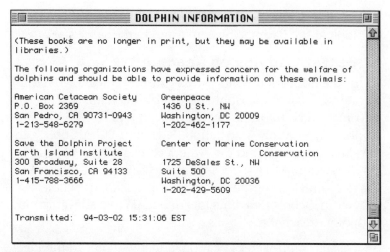

```
═╬╗■       DOLPHIN INFORMATION       ═══════╗╤
(These books are no longer in print, but they may be available in
libraries.)

The following organizations have expressed concern for the welfare of
dolphins and should be able to provide information on these animals:

American Cetacean Society      Greenpeace
P.O. Box 2369                  1436 U St., NW
San Pedro, CA 90731-0943       Washington, DC 20009
1-213-548-6279                 1-202-462-1177

Save the Dolphin Project       Center for Marine Conservation
Earth Island Institute                    Conservation
300 Broadway, Suite 28         1725 DeSales St., NW
San Francisco, CA 94133        Suite 500
1-415-788-3666                 Washington, DC 20036
                               1-202-429-5609

Transmitted:  94-03-02 15:31:06 EST
```

Figure 6.5 *One of the Geographic Information Files, concerning dolphins*

- If kids want to write riddles and solve them, have them click Kid's World.

- To get suggestions for curriculum, click Curriculum Projects.

- For articles and workshops of interest to teachers, click Professional Conferences.

Getting Advice on Parenting

America Online put this collection of forums together: Type the Keyword Education, scroll down the list on the right, and double click Parents' Information Network to meet with other parents and experts on subjects such as adoption, child abuse, giftedness, home schooling, Montessori schooling, study skills, special education, and substance abuse.

- To swap advice and stories about premature babies, preschoolers, and software for parents, click Parents' Exchange inside the Parents' Information Network window.

- For hints about other parent services on AOL, take a look at the Parents' System Map, in the same spot.

Getting Advice on Teaching

In the Education window (Keyword: Education), scroll through the list at the right and double-click the Teachers' Information Network to tap into forums run by the National Education Association (Keyword: NEA Public). In the same list you'll find the American Federation of Teachers (Keyword: AFT), the Association for Supervision and Curriculum Development (Keyword: ASCD), or Scholastic (Keyword: Scholastic), plus lots of boards to trade shop talk with other teachers.

- Discuss high-tech education, and swap files in the Electronic Schoolhouse and Multimedia Exchange.
- Get lesson plans from the Lesson Plan Libraries.
- Scan for possible funding in the Grant Chest.
- Attend a seminar with other teachers in the Teachers' University (it's free).

Looking Up Educational Research and Advice

The Educational Research Information Clearinghouse, known colloquially as ERIC, has gone online.

From the ERIC Window, you can get information about various online databases or libraries devoted to education, institutes that do educational research, upcoming teacher conferences, news about ERIC itself, and digests of experts' opinions (although I'd say some of these digests are short because they reflect shallow thinking and thin research). Essentially, ERIC is a resource for teachers, but parents can learn a lot, looking over the wall.

1. **Choose Keyword from the Go To menu, and type ERIC.**

   You see the AskERIC window, with icons for its message center, databases, and a set of prepared answers to the most-often asked questions. In a scrolling list, you see the kind of information you can receive (Figure 6.6).

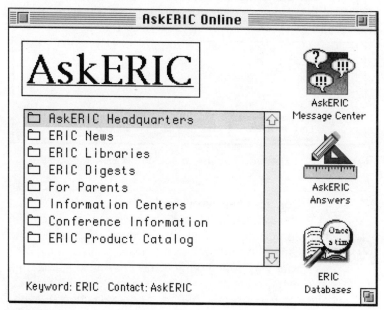

Figure 6.6   *The AskERIC window*

2. **To search the database for brief articles on a particular subject, click ERIC Databases, select Search AskERIC Online, type your topic, and click whatever sources you think might provide the information (Figure 6.7). Then click List Articles.**

```
┌─────────────────────────────────────────────────────┐
│ ▤▣       Search AskERIC                            ▣ │
├─────────────────────────────────────────────────────┤
│  Search AskERIC                                       │
│                                                       │
│  Type words that describe what you are looking for, then click List Articles. You │
│  may narrow your search by clicking on one or more of the categories. Click on     │
│  Help & Info for more instructions.                   │
│                                                       │
│  ☐ AskERIC Answers    ☐ AskERIC News    ☐ ERIC Digests │
│  ☐ Information Centers ☐ Conference Info ☐ For Parents │
│  ┌───────────────────────────────────────────────┐   │
│  │ |                                             │   │
│  └───────────────────────────────────────────────┘   │
│  ┌─────────────────────────────────────────────┬─┐   │
│  │                                             │⇧│   │
│  │                                             │ │   │
│  │                                             │ │   │
│  │                                             │ │   │
│  │                                             │⇩│   │
│  └─────────────────────────────────────────────┴─┘   │
│  ┌──────────────┐ ┌─────────┐ ┌───────────────┐      │
│  │ List Articles│ │  More   │ │  Help & Info  │   ▨  │
│  └──────────────┘ └─────────┘ └───────────────┘      │
└─────────────────────────────────────────────────────┘
```

Figure 6.7   *The form you use to search the ERIC database*

 Consider the scrolling list. If you want to find out about dozens of special institutes dedicated in some way or other to education, double-click the listing for Information Centers, and double-click your way down to the actual information about one of these centers. To get advice on parenting, open the For Parents subdirectory. To locate some free and some cheap publications, explore the ERIC Product Catalog.

---

3. Double-click any article listed to see it (Figure 6.8).

4. To preserve the article, choose Save, Print, or Print Text from the File menu.

Taking a Class

If your local community college or university extension has a course, you'll probably find it offered in The Online Campus, one of the main features in the Education department. (It's listed under T for The.)

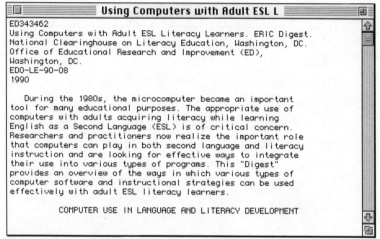

Figure 6.8 *Typical article from ERIC*

 Basically, you skim through the catalog, pick a course, register, and then get a confirmation note telling you when the class will meet online. When you sign on at that time, you "go" to the classroom to have an online conversation with the instructor and other students. Then you download homework assignments, browse the reference section of the library, do the assignments, and upload your answers for the instructor to grade. And so it goes for four to eight weeks, usually, for about $20 a class.

1. On the Go To menu, choose Keyword, and type in IES, for Interactive Education System.

2. Go to the IES Registration Center, and open the Online Catalog. Open a department to see its courses (Figure 6.9).

3. Read about a course and its instructor.

4. In Windows, click Registration on the Mac, open the Registration folder, or the Early Registration folder, and sign up.

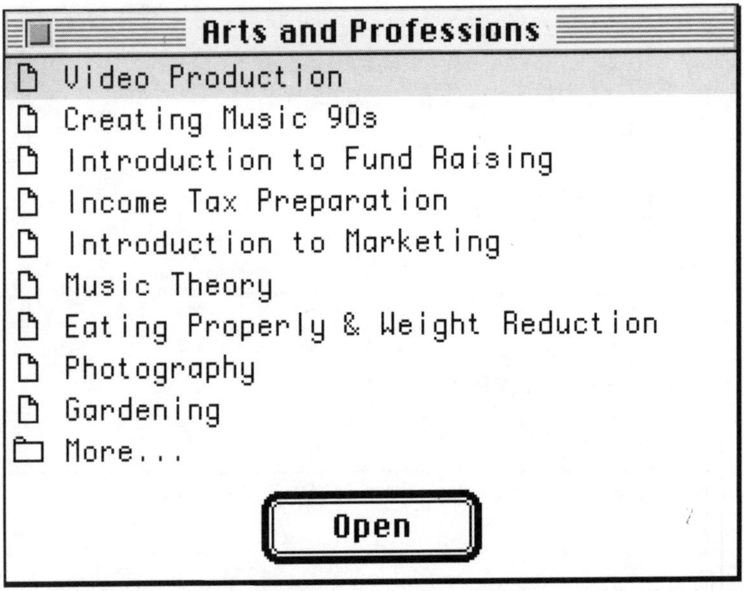

Figure 6.9 *Here are the courses offered in Arts and Professions*

5. **When you receive confirmation, sign on at the right time, and go to the classroom.**

   The instructor conducts an online discussion, goes over the homework, tells you where to find the reference material in the library, and explains how you can get in touch personally, for office hours.

6. **Then, after class, download the homework assignment and the reference material for the next week.**

7. **Finally, to relax, go to one of the off-campus hangouts, such as the Bull Moose Tavern (to talk history and politics), or the Afterwards Cafe (art and theater), or test your knowledge in an academic contest in the Coliseum.**

Getting Help with Homework, and Plans for College

The Academic Assistance Center offers all kinds of support for harried students.

1. **Choose Keyword from the GoTo menu, and type Homework.**

   You'll see the list of services.

   • **If you want help with a particular subject,** click the Academic Assistance icon, and double-click one of the subject rooms (Figure 6.10).

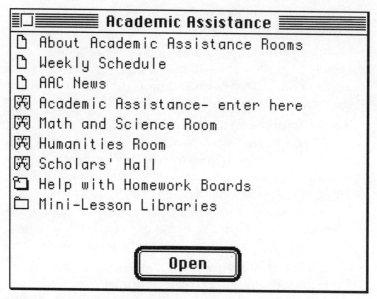

Figure 6.10 *You can get help in the subject rooms*

If you have a specific question, go to the Homework Help Board and post it there. AOL has volunteers who tour these boards and reply quickly. Often, they forward your question to an expert in the field. Cruise back by in a day or so to see what responses turn up. Or click the Teacher Pager, to see if anyone is free right now.

- **If you want to learn to study more efficiently,** check out the Study Skills Service. These folks make a living teaching kids how to study; they promise you'll spend less time, and learn more, if you do what they say.

- **Facing exams?** Get tips on test taking, browse through a list of the toughest questions in every field (with the answers), look at dozens of actual exams in your field, and—every night during exam season—chat with pros in the Exam Prep Center. These sessions really help you think through what you're facing. For instance, a teacher put the following sentence in front of the students: Tomorrow we will buy 20 pizzas. Can you spot the subject? The predicate? Radical!

- **Facing a research problem?** Can't get to the library? A bunch of professors will point you toward the right books, and, if there's an online forum, tell you about that, too. See the Online Research Service.

- **Need crib notes on a classic?** Barron's Booknotes notes have been posted here. Written by starving grad students, these notes represent what an energetic undergraduate might find in many hours of hard work; here, you can download the whole booklet, and print it out. The prose is too fancy to steal directly, but the notes can probably help you make sense out of a book in which the style stands between you and the meaning.

- **Want to trade notes with other students?** Read articles from college newspapers; sell computer games to other students; swap files such as a list of English teaching jobs in Japan; find out how to study abroad, get discounts on books; and get help from the rebellious *Princeton Review,* which offers lots of tips for cracking the college board exams, in Student Access Online, inside the Academic Assistance folder.

- **Need the official line on the College Boards?** This forum offers a superficial tour of financial aid (gosh, you may have to take a part-time job!), sample tests, videos for sale, and best of all, a board in which you can hear what other students have to say. Naturally, it's called Ask the College Board. If college is in your future (or your kid's future), you probably ought to check out this forum, for the party line about the SAT and achievement tests. But for more helpful info, I recommend the *Princeton Review* over in Student Access Online.

CHAPTER 7

Chatting

Through America Online there are areas such as the People Connection, in which you can type directly to other people while they type back to you. Informally known as chatting, this kind of exchange resembles the old-fashioned telegraph—you type, then the other guy types, then you type, and so on. But in some chat rooms there may be two dozen people all typing away. Advantages: You don't have to wait more than a few seconds for a response, you can build on that response without waiting a week, you can progress from a general conversation in which many people participate to a private conversation. Disadvantages: You can't hear anyone's voice, you can't see them, and those other conversations do occasionally get in the way.

For example, if you need help on homework, you can get it at the Academic Assistance Center (Keyword: Homework), in a room with two or three volunteer instructors and a dozen or more other students, all talking at once, and all getting answers. Of course, when one of the instructors sees a need, he or she initiates a conversation offline, with an Instant Message, in which the two of you can type in private. Meanwhile, you'll notice that the same instructor is answering other questions in the main room. If you've never tried this kind of conversation, you probably think it'd be like trying to discuss Shakespeare in a loud disco, but actually you can follow the various threads fairly easily after a few moments.

Going into one of the chat rooms is like wearing a mask and costume to a ball. Your screen name is there, but unless you've spelled out your complete life history in your member profile, no one can find out anything about you, unless you want them to: Your face, your figure, your address, your ordinary personality are all hidden from the others online. The People Connection lets you make social contact with folks you'd never meet in real life; it's a party by proxy, dating at arm's length, schmoozing without the water cooler.

Starting at the Lobby

One way to start visiting is to go to the Lobby, a vague landing spot from which corridors upon corridors of rooms open up, leading you into more meetings than a hotel can offer during a convention. After all, there are more than half-a-million folks out there, and in the last year, they've doubled the number of times they dial in. They're not all doing this for serious business reasons; some are here to schmooze, titillate, or get psychic readings!

1. **Choose Lobby on the Go To menu.**
   If someone has taken that command off your Go To menu, choose Keyword from the Go To menu, and type Lobby. You see a Lobby window (during rush hour, AOL opens many lobbies) (Figure 7.1). First timers may go to the New Members Lounge.

2. **Adjust your conversation or find out more about the other people there.**
   In Windows, double-click a name in the list at the top. Then find out more about that person by clicking Get Info; send a message by clicking Message, or, if you want that person's comments removed, click Ignore.

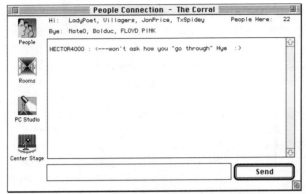

Figure 7.1 *The Lobby is the starting point on your visit to the chat rooms*

On the Mac, click People, select a person's screen name, and then, to find out more, click Get Info; to send a private e-mail, click Message; to boldface their lines, click Highlight; or to excise their lines, click Ignore.

3. **To find out what chat rooms are open, click List Rooms in Windows or Rooms on the Mac (Figure 7.2).**

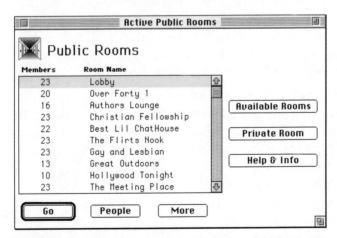

Figure 7.2 *To see who's in a public room, click People. To see more public rooms, click More. To see which chat rooms actually have room for another member, click Available Rooms. To create a private room, click Private Room, give it a name, and go there.*

Beyond the Lobby are regularly scheduled chat rooms, such as the Best Lil' Chat House; public rooms that have been invented on the spur of the moment, but are open to any member, until they reach 23 attendees; and then very private rooms. You can create a private room in order to have a real-time chat with friends all over the country. Only you and they know the name.

Here are some samples of people chatting online:

```
First: She's in the hospital right now.
Second: Sorry to hear that, Bill. Hope
    she's OK.
First: Silly, isn't it?
Second: OK, First, is there anything you
    need to know before we start?
First: Yes.
Third: Hello. What is this line all
    about? I'm new to this.
Fourth: Hi, Third. We sometimes get card
    readings. There's one going on now.
Third: Why isn't anyone talking? Did I
    interrupt?
Fifth: The screen seems very slow
    tonight.
Third: Can I get a card reading?
Second: Yes, have to wait turn. :)
Third: OK:(
```

```
Newcomer: IS THIS THE AUTHOR'S LOUNGE?
    DO YOU WRITE OR WHAT?
Second: First take off your caps.
Third: We're still trying to figure it
    out.
Fourth: Final Gifts is a good one.
Fifth: We all write. Read the screen.
First: HUH?
```

Sixth: Newcomer...first things
  first...that little button..."
  Capslock"...try pushing that sucker!
Seventh: <—away from keyboard
Newcomer: OK, Sixth...are you happy?
Eighth: All, good eve ;)

First: Anyone in CA?
Second: So I said, Naw. :(
First: Just talking to someone in CA,
  line went dead.
Second: You think it's a quake?
Third: No shaker here in San Diego.
Fourth: All calm in SF.
First: Just wondering.
Fifth: Radio says power outages here in
  Burbank. Aftershock.
Second: Now the phone lines'll be
  jammed.
First: Any other news? How big?
Fifth: Not very. Your friend's probably
  OK. They
First: Good.
Fifth: run powerlines on poles, and the
  poles come down.

First: Shame on you! Take your blouse
  off.
Second: Good subs are so hard to find.
Third: Aren't they!
First: Third, are you dom?
Second: Interested?
Fourth: Yes, mistress. My face is red
  and I am so afraid someone will come
  in the room.
Second: I hate shy subs, don't you?
First: There are 12 people in the room.
  They are here to see you serve me.

Exploring the Rooms Systematically

Going into the Lobby and "walking around" is a fine way
to get a sampling of chats available in the People Connection. But that ambling-around can be confusing, and if you
come on a busy night, many chats turn out to be filled with
people. (The limit's about two dozen people per room.)
Here's a way to get a complete list of the chats that are
scheduled on a regular basis in People Connection:

1. **Go to the Lobby and choose PC Studio.**

2. **Double-click People Connection Events.**

3. **To see lists of regular chats, double-click Event Rooms
   Guide and open one of the groups.**

   You get a rundown on the supposed topic, time, and
   location.

 This list includes only chats set up in the People
Connection. There are many more chats throughout
AOL, in various departments and forums. Keep your
eye out, everywhere, for icons that read "Talk
with," or something like that.

4. **To look at a complete schedule of chats for the week,
   go to the Lobby, click PC Studio, click People Connection Events, and then open Event Rooms Schedule.**

 Event Rooms is just a fancy name for rooms you
can chat in—public or private. Don't hold your
breath, in most of them, for some big event.

Joining the Conversation

Generally, wait a little to see what is going on, if anything.
Say hello when you come in. Feel free to ask about all the
acronyms and local slang. Don't type in all uppercase:
That's too loud.

1. To send a message, type it, and then click Send.

You don't need to keep waiting for an opening. There's a few-second delay built into the whole setup. Watch your message appear and slide up the screen. See if anyone responds. Turn your attention to anyone who does.

2. Keep sending.

Don't give up. If at first the conversation seems to be going on without you, it is; people are finishing what they started before you arrived. Persist.

Using Smileys and Shorthand

Because most of us hate to type, we use shorthand—abbreviations for common phrases—and because we can't wave hello, we use smileys—gestures suggested by playing around with punctuation. Tilt your head to the left to see most of these; for instance, meet Mr. Smileyface ;)

Here are some common abbreviations and acronyms:

afk	Away from keyboard
bak	Back at keyboard
brb	Be right back
btw	By the way
cul8r	See you later
gmta	Great minds think alike
lol	Laughing out loud
otf	On the floor (laughing)
rotf	Rolling on the floor
roflwtime	Rolling on floor with tears in my eyes
ttfn	Ta-ta for now!
wb	Welcome back
wtg	Way to go

Here are some other common smileys:

:-)	Just joking
:D	Broad grin
:*	Kiss
:X	My lips are sealed

:P	Sticking out tongue (Bronx cheer)
{}	A hug (you can put someone's name inside)
:(	Sad look, frown
:-!	Foot in mouth
:-$	Put your money where your mouth is
<:-)	Don't blame me, I'm a dunce
C:-)	Blame me, I'm an egghead
8:-)	Sent by a little girl
:-)===	Sent by a giraffe
d:-)	I like to play baseball
:-{}	I have a mustache
:-&	I'm tongue-tied
:-	Male
>-	Female

Preserving a Log of the Conversation

You can save fascinating chats, just in case you want to review them.

1. **In Windows, choose Logging. On the Mac, choose Logs from the File menu.**

2. **Select Chat, click Open, and then specify where to save the log.**

   You can reread the file later, using Open from the File menu.

If You Missed a Session

You can get a transcript of certain chats—generally those that offer a lot of advice. The transcript, known as a log, may be a crude ASCII text file with odd line breaks and occasional gaps, or it may be a carefully edited, easy-to-print file.

1. **Go to the Lobby, choose PC Studio, and double-click People Connection Events.**

2. **Open the Event Library.**

3. **Skim through the list of logs using the More button, then select the one you want and click Open.**

If You'd Like to Host a Room

You can come up with an idea for a new chat room, or you can offer to act as a host for a room that's already under way. You have to have been an AOL member for six months, without any payment problems, or "violations of the Terms of Service," whatever that means.

1. **Go to the Lobby, choose PC Studio, and double-click People Connection Events.**
2. **Open the Event Library.**
3. **Download the New Room Proposal or Event Host Application.**
4. **Return these forms to the screen names suggested, but do so as e-mail, not a file.**

Adding Sounds

You can send and receive sounds, just as you do words. If you're using a Mac, just choose Sound on the Chat menu and pick a sound to send.

For a PC, you need a speaker and some speaker software (you can download Speak.exe from a Windows forum). Collect some sounds ending in .wav from Windows forums (Keyword: PC Music) and put them in your WAOL directory.

Downside: Most people without Macs are still not multimedia-ready, so your sounds will be lost on them.

Looking at Pictures of Fellow Chatters

Some members send in their pictures so you can get an idea of the person you're chatting with. AOL scans these snapshots and posts them for you to flip through—they call it the Gallery.

1. **Go to the Lobby, and choose PC Studio.**
2. **Open the Gallery, and skim through the collection:**
- To see who's new, open New Files.
- To see other members, open the Portrait Galleries.

- To see pictures of family members, open Additional Gallery Libraries and look at the Family Album.

- To see pictures of AOL staffers, open the Additional Gallery Libraries and look at the Rogues' Gallery.

3. Download the file.

The file may be in Graphic Image Format (GIF), an all-purpose format.

4. Use a GIF converter or viewer to look at the picture, or convert it to another graphic format you can use in your graphic software.

 Open the GIF Viewers directory for tips on software you can use to view these pictures directly, or to convert them into a format you can use in other graphic software.

Customizing the Way Your Chats Go

You can adjust the way chats appear on your screen by using the Preferences command on the Chat menu. While you're looking at preferences, consider all the other kinds: You can display in any font you want. On Windows, you can have the people in the room listed alphabetically or in their order of appearance.

Making a Personal Call (Instant Message)

In a larger chat room you may find someone you're sympatico with. If you feel like it, you can send an Instant Message directly to anyone who is online at the same time. That way, you can say something personal, or suggest you go off to a new private room (invent the name and then create it) for a chat no one else can overhear.

1. **Choose Send Instant Message from the Members menu (Figure 7.3).**

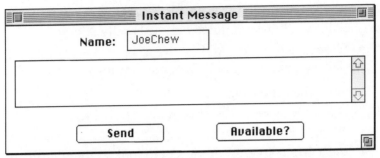

Figure 7.3 *You can type an instant message and send it directly to someone who is online right now. If in doubt, click Available to see if the member's still online.*

2. Type in the screen name of the recipient, the message, and send it on its way.

Finding Out What's Happening

1. For a schedule of regular chats, choose Keyword from the Go To menu, type PC Studio, and then double-click People Connection Events or, as it's sometimes known, What's Happening This Week (Figure 7.4).

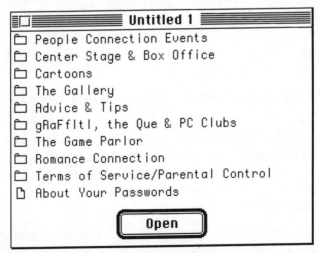

Figure 7.4 *People Connection Studio lists some of what's happening*

2. For big events in which you sit in rows in a big audience and get to ask questions of someone famous, open Center Stage.

3. To find folks looking for romance, open Romance Connection, pick an age group, and skim the subjects to see if anyone interests you.

 At least one long-distance romance has ended in marriage—in a private chat room. More blissful messages appear in the HappyEndings board in Romance Connection.

Setting Up and Using a Private Room

If you want to meet with some friends to type over some thoughts, tell them a time and an unusual name (one that no one else will try to use). Then sign on early, go to the lobby (Keyword: Lobby), and click Rooms.

1. **Click Private Rooms.**

2. **Type the name of your private room.**

   It is created, and you go right to it. Now everyone else can sign on the same way you created it, and you'll be able to type back and forth without being bothered by anyone else.

PART III

What You'll Find Online

In this part of the book, we'll hike up the most interesting mountains in AOL (the mountains are called departments), look at the high points, and then visit some of the big tourist attractions on the way back down.

 Sometimes you'll get the feeling that a service or forum you really like has moved. Actually, what's happened is that the same forum has been advertised on two lists at once. For instance, you may find the Compton's Online Encyclopedia in Education, Kids Only, and the Reference Desk. Similarly, some magazines show up all around the net and then appear in a big list in The Newsstand.

Change is also a part of every forum. The staff is always busy. They change the names of forums, they change the icons, they change the way topics are organized. When a particular thread of conversation seems to have reached a conclusion, the host may yank it from the message board and preserve it in the forum's archives. Everyone who runs a forum, it seems, likes to tinker. So by the time you read this, you'll find small changes have overtaken what I say; for instance, the Traveler's Corner may have become the Traveler's Suitcase. You won't get badly lost when you encounter these transformations, but just as in a meadow you walk through over and over, you'll notice a constant interplay of stirrings, ripples, and settlings with new growth, clearings, and subtle shifts in color.

Gradually, you'll chip chunks of wood out of the trees along the trail you like best and go back over those trails so often you become familiar with the slightest changes along the way.

Unlike a word processing application, which stays pretty much the way you bought it until you go out and buy an update, America Online just keeps growing. That's part of the excitement, but it's sometimes a cause of confusion: When you read one of the chapters here, you'll know the most important features of a department, but you'll want to keep coming back to any department you're interested in, just to see what the staff has planted this week. And with the onrush of hundreds of thousands of new members, you can be sure that even the tiniest sub-sub-subforum will attract newcomers who shake up the message boards, posting new questions, taking controversial positions, and generally making it worth a return visit in a few days.

Here's a glimpse of the territory we're going to cover:

Clubs and Interests

Computing

Education

Entertainment

Internet Connection

Kids Only

Marketplace

Newsstand

People Connection

Personal Finance

Reference Desk

Sports

Today's News

Travel

Member Services

And, of course, within a month or two, there'll be more! That's what makes America Online so much fun to explore, over and over.

CHAPTER **8**

Clubs
and Interests

In this department, you can meet like-minded folks who are interested in the same subjects you enjoy. You can read what they have to say, post your own views, and participate in shared events. Many of these areas involve hobbies such as astronomy, aviation, genealogy, ham radio, photography, radio-controlled vehicles, Scuba diving, even *Star Trek.* Other areas involve discussions of more serious subjects, such as business and finance, cooking, disabilities, emergency response, the environment, ethics and religion, gay and lesbian issues, mental health, the military, the space program, pet care, and senior issues.

Here's a sampling of the forums in Clubs & Interests, along with the keywords that take you directly to a special interest:

Forum	Keywords
Asimov/Analog Forum	asimov, analog
Astronomy Club	astronomy
Aviation Club	aviation
Baby Boomers Club	baby boomers
Better Health & Medical Forum	health
Bicycle Network, The	bikenet, bicycle
Business & Finance	business
Business Strategies	business strategies
Chicago Online	chicago online
Cooking Club	cooking
DisABILITIES Forum	disabilities
Dolby Audio/Video Forum	dolby
Emergency Response Club	emergency
Environmental Forum	environment
Ethics and Religion Forum	religion
Exchange, The	the exchange
Express Yourself	debate
Gadget Guru Electronics Forum	electronics
Gay & Lesbian Forum	gay, lesbian
Genealogy Club	genealogy
Grandstand, The	grandstand
Ham Radio Club	ham radio
Hatrack River Town Meeting	orson scott card, hatrack
Issues in Mental Health	imh
Military and Vets Club	military
National Space Society	nss, space
Online Gaming Forums	gaming, ogf
Pet Care Club	pet care
Photography Forum	photography, kodak
Real Estate Online	real estate, mls, mortgage rates
Rocklink	rocklink
Science Fiction Forum	science fiction
Scuba Club	scuba
SeniorNet	seniornet
Sports Link	sports
Star Trek Club	star trek
Student Access Online	student
Trivia Club	trivia
Wine & Dine Online	wine, restaurant, beer
Writers Club	writers

Astronomy Club

OK, so I expected a bunch of nerds hogging the telescope during the eclipse. Mr. Astro is the club host (actually, an editor at *Sky and Telescope* magazine) and he and the other members tell you how to spot missing galaxies, track comets, follow the movement of planets, and look for the hot events in your local sky.

If you're still upset about the problems with the Hubble Space Telescope, this is the place to vent your concerns. (Go to Cosmic Discussions.) You can download photographs of newly discovered supernovas and Ida's moon (an asteroid with a satellite!).

Aviation

Flying (it's a magazine) has gone online. If you're interested in a piston-powered twin-engine craft, you'll find articles on the last company producing them. Plus personal stories (ice on the wings and slush in the wheels); challenges (if you have a 747 with a load of pigeons and they all take off at once . . .); messages about spare parts, technique, and news about personal planes. I was glad to see two articles about the Mustang, the plane my father used to have when we flew from Maine to Minnesota to see the headwaters of the Mississippi. This forum's a down-home place to land, if you fly. And if you prefer programs like Microsoft's Flight Simulator, you can join three simulated airlines, flying with timetables, scenery, and, of course, IFR (the rules that apply when you have to fly by instruments because you can't see more than 20 feet out the window). You download advice, scenery, and control panels for different planes.

Baby Boomers

Here's a club for anyone born from 1945 to 1969. Reminisce about Beatles' concerts, Led Zep, and Jean Shepherd. Debate whether Frank Zappa should be hailed as a genius because he invented the Fuzz-Wah pedal and fought censorship in Congress. His dental floss ranch will live forever. And, once you've heard her story, you'll never forget Suzy Creamcheese.

You can get teary over memories of old TV and movies, too. Sing the Mickey Mouse song again. From *I Love Lucy* through *Dallas,* you can moan and groan and wonder where they went. Were you watching when Soupy Sales told all us kids to go into the bedroom, get Dad's wallet, and send Soupy all those green pieces of paper?

Backpackers and Bike Enthusiasts

We had to stop by the *Backpacker Magazine* area to register at the trailhead and celebrate National Trails Day (2,000 events, with 2,500 organizations!). Keyword: Backpacker.

Campaign against 4WD vehicles in commercials when they slew off the road and rip up tundra or destroy fragile streambeds, just to get mud flashing into the camera. Get tips on what to do with empty 35mm film canisters and Q-Tips. What's great is these folks have actually been out on the trail and know the problems behind the ad copy. They offer Trailside TV, with a show about a bike trip through the California redwoods—a strenuous pedal, with 20% grades. I've hiked the Appalachian Trail in the White Mountains, and I was glad to see these folks have done a video about that, calling it the toughest mile in the Trail. Now which one was that? As is appropriate for a hut up in the mountains, they have a tiny store, selling their magazine and a few key items for swatting mosquitoes.

Bicycling Magazine has its own booth, too, with articles about big butt syndrome (yes, your bottom can spread if you keep riding your bike all day), news about upcoming races, software you can download (see the Tour de France route), shareware images (see the German team in front of an Alpine inn), databases of information from old issues, and a database of product information.

BikeNet—another forum next door to the magazine—offers a meeting place for a lot of organizations wheeling and dealing with bikes. Some celebrate Bikecentennial. Slogan: "Informed Cyclists Want to Know."

Express Yourself

In the Express Yourself area, you can send e-mail directly to the president (Keyword: White House), browse through material the White House staff has posted about the budget, economy, education, and so on, exchange views with other members about foreign policy ("What Foreign Policy?"), and (don't miss this!) contemporary journalism (Media Watch). The comments are more interesting than the columnists in the paper. You can even get complete transcripts of presidential news conferences, briefings, town hall meetings, and talking papers from the Download library.

The Michigan governor has set up a similar forum, as have the *New Republic* and AOL itself, in the Issues and Debate Forum. Exciting personal attacks, a little fire and brimstone, and lots of good ideas from policy wonks, little people, and occasionally the Veep himself.

Focus Groups

A company called BKG Youth carries out marketing focus groups online, hosting a session in which a dozen or so folks, carefully chosen to fit the profile of potential customers, answer questions about what they like and don't like in competitive products. If you participate, you might get some free products, or cash (Keyword: Dialogue). The main focus is teens, so pimple cream and cosmetics rate high on the current list of assignments.

Fill out the form and sign up. Answer the surveys to get an idea of what marketing folks see as big new trends. "Are our forecasted trends on target? Are you experiencing things like these in your life?" For only $397 a year, you can get the conclusions BKG comes to, in its magazine, titled (no kidding!) *nachur of realitees*.

Kodak Photography Forum

From snapshots to digital imaging, this forum lets you chat with other photographers, and Ron Baird, who speaks for Kodak (and goes out to find answers to your questions, deep in Rochester). There are heaps of postings about Kodak's PhotoCD (no, they haven't ironed out all the kinks, but it's pretty hot anyway), outdoor photography, wedding photography, and modeling (male photographers are beginning to insist on having a third person present during what they call boudoir photo sessions, to avoid being charged with harassment). Advertise equipment to buy, sell, or swap, and pick up utilities for doing digital imaging.

Science Fiction

If you like fantasy, horror, mystery, *Star Wars*, "Star Trek", or other science fiction, blast off for the keyword Science Fiction. Here you can learn what's coming on the SciFi Channel and who did what in *Mad* Magazine or *Vertigo* (click the DC Comics icon in the Science Fiction window).

Omni Magazine has staked out a major booth here (Keyword: Omni). The editor boasts that William Gibson used the term *cyberspace* in their magazine years before he published *Neuromancer,* and, somehow, the *Omni* area's supposed to occur in that otherworldly environment. The staff and readers have really gotten into swapping bios, dreams, complaints, suspicions, and reminiscences of their last voyage in alien spaceships. Seems as if every author of a major piece comes on for a discussion (check What's Happening). The bulletin boards discuss the paranormal from aliens to UFOs (AntiMatter); articles cover a woman who "channels" the voice of Barbie; and you can branch out to samples from *Compute,* another Omni magazine.

Neat corner of the *Omni* realm: Click the icon called SF/Fantasy World and enter Ellen Datlow's environment, in which she encourages people to write science fiction and post it for each other to read (Figure 8.1).

Figure 8.1   *SF/Fantasy World*

The Writer's Club and Hatrack

You can join the National Writer's Union, a wonderful if quixotic endeavor; it provides good advice about contracts, and a forum in which to grouse. In the forums, meet folks interested in Arthurian legends and work together to create a progressive story, craft romantic marriage proposals, erotica, technical writing, online help, hypertext, fairy tales, hypertext fiction, and ethnic fiction of all shades. The union offers its own bulletin board here.

If you like to write a blend of historical romance, fantasy, and science fiction visit the early 19th-century environment of Hatrack River (Keyword: Hatrack), launched by Orson Scott Card. It's an imaginary town, born after America lost its revolution, so England sends its magically gifted over to Hatrack River—and you're invited to play a part as a citizen. You can read what other folks say, then join in. It's a communal work, growing as people come and go, orchestrated and guided by the original vision of one author, but weaving together hundreds of voices. Meet the blacksmith, basket weaver, woodworker, and taleswapper.

CHAPTER **9**

Computing and Software

Here's where to go for a ton of downloadable software, lots of gossip about tomorrow's news, plenty of advice from other members, support from vendors, and big-time conferences with visiting celebrities in the computer business.

What you actually see when you enter this department depends on what computer you're using. When you dial in, AOL recognizes your operating system and displays a special set of icons and list of forums advertising information relevant to your operating system. Basic to the department, no matter what system you are using, are several icons on the left, devoted to:

- One or more magazines devoted to that operating system
- A software center full of shareware, utilities, demos, and sample files
- An Industry Connection for talking to the reps of the people who sold you your machine and programs
- News and Reference, with short stories about recent developments and customer support databases

If you have several different computers, you can browse this department for information about DOS, Windows, OS/2, Apple II, and Macintosh programs, no matter what machine you use to enter the Computing and Software department. All that AOL does is to show you the material about the operating system you're using to dial in; but you can always look up everything else, too. There are 50,000 files out there, just waiting for you!

On the right you'll see a scrolling list of forums, devoted to topics such as Beginners, Development, Hardware, Music & Sound, and more. Each forum has its own message boards, upload and download areas, and special activities such as contests.

Software Center

For each operating system, this is a central collection point for all the applicatons, utilities, patches, and updates that appear separately out in the forum libraries. (You can use the Search Software Libraries on the Go To menu to find a file no matter which forum library it may live in.) Here are some of the files you may want to collect:

- Art in many different file formats, commercial and amateur—photos, drawings, logos, movies, and startup screens
- Conference transcripts from each forum (for example, a talk by a leading Ethernet guru, in the Communications forum)
- Demonstration software—it looks like the real thing, it is the real thing, except, well, you probably can't save a file, or print
- Fonts—some great bargains here, in free- or shareware, compared to the cost of new fonts from the major vendors (I like Chaucer, an ornamental drop-cap; Boswell, a reconstruction of the 18th century font used in one of Boswell's books, so accurate it reproduces the defects; and Phoenician, for all your papyrus scrolls)

If you do desktop publishing, get PostScript fonts, sometimes listed as Type 1 or Type 2 or ATM for Adobe Type Manager; if you don't have to print crisply at any resolution, you might as well choose TrueType fonts, which work fine on dot matrix, inkjet, or laser printers.

- Macros, scripts, tools, plug-ins—extra modules that make your software jump through hoops in new ways
- New files of different types, usually from the last week or so; helpful if you've already browsed through all the old files and just want to look at the new stuff
- Sound files (oinks, squawks, songs, and beeps)
- Source code for you to tweak, if you're a developer
- Technical notes from vendors showing developers how to use their languages, utilities, compilers, or conversion routines
- Templates—if you have the software, the template does half the work for you, setting up a form for you to fill in
- Top this-and-that—basically, the most popular downloads from each area
- Updates to your current software, patches, and bug fixes
- Utilities that compress files, convert files from one format to another, and play files without your having the original program

Some of my favorite downloads: Mac software to help you name your new rock 'n' roll group (Band-O-Matic); in the Windows specialty library called Earth, Planets, and Space, software for tracking hurricanes (Storm); and in the Home and Hobby Helpers for Windows, BABYSITR, which preserves everything you ever thought to tell the babysitter, ready to print out and post on the fridge; and, of course, GROCER, which prompts you for everything you usually forget to buy at the supermarket. Who can deny that AOL is educational!

Industry Connection

For support, gossip, conferences, and conversation organized around those vendors who create your hardware and software, click Industry Connection on your main Computing and Software window. You see a window like the one shown in Figure 8.1.

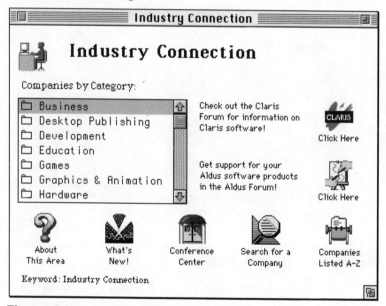

Figure 9.1   *Industry Connection window*

The companies featured on the main window change from month to month, depending on which one's pushing hardest for promotion; usually, these companies are major players. Claris, which is anxious to play in both the Mac and Windows worlds, has placed its icon here this month. When you click its icon, you get—after a slight delay—a fairly typical big-company window, shown in Figure 8.2.

Here are six areas that commonly appear in a vendor's window. To find out about their products, click Product Information; you get data sheets and press releases in these areas, plus occasional demos.

Figure 9.2 *The Claris window*

If you have a problem and want to ask a user group or post a message specifically for the vendor's tech support team, click Technical Support. Keep an eye out for any folder that has a name such as Frequently Asked Questions—it contains the answers developed by the folks on the hotline. Often your problems can be resolved right there.

Similarly, if the company puts up a database of technical information, take the time to search it; often the vendor has collected all the "answers" created by the hotline people and put them all in a searchable database. That database is what they use when you call on the phone. But you can use it now, here on AOL.

Another area offers Customer Service, an ambiguous term encompassing direct sales, sales of support, and lists of support numbers.

There's usually a software library for patches, upgrades, big fixes, and extra templates that help you out if you already have the company's software; for instance, in the Claris Software Library, under FileMaker Pro, I found a database already set for my home inventory for insurance purposes, and I found a Personal Librarian as a way of tracking my books. Major vendors gather these "extras" from eager users, vet them for bugs, and then redistribute them to encourage other users to keep using their products. Enlightened self-interest.

Finally, if you've got a bright idea, or an outstanding complaint, take advantage of the Suggestion Box.

Technology News and Resources

You can locate great magazines and databases full of little details you didn't know you needed in the Resource Center, also known as News and Reference. Click the icon on the Computing window, then decide whether you want to look at publications, databases, or backup resources.

Craig Crossman runs a national radio show about computers; his online forum tells you how to locate a station that carries him, provides the next month of shows, offers a board in which you can chat with him (he actually checks in every day and responds), and rewards you with a lot of prizes. Craig appears in the list of publications.

The CyberLaw database sounds like RoboCop Goes to Court, but this column started at Stanford University and spread to the big user groups around the country. These folks report legal issues that touch the computer industry: copyright questions, privacy issues, information theft, programming freedom, all the lawsuits about "look and feel," and the FBI's push to make phone companies change their digital switching systems (carrying on and off signals only) to make them stupider so that the FBI can continue to wiretap now that the phone lines are no longer analog (carrying waves of sound). You can also post messages as part of an ongoing discussion with the creator of CyberLaw, Jonathan Rosenoer.

If you are wondering what a computer term means, try the database called The Dictionary of Computer Terms. Just don't ask about anything that refers to current issues in the industry, such as hypertext, electronic performance support systems, or the Standard Generalized Mark Up Language (SGML). No articles were found for those topics.

If you rely on a Microsoft product, check out its database called Knowledge Base for answers to key questions. This is the database Microsoft's support people use as their first attempt to solve your problem. Here's a problem that has existed in Word since its first release almost ten years ago. You assign a style (or format) to a paragraph. Later, you select the paragraph and assign another style to it. Nothing happens. Or that paragraph and all others in the same style turn into boldface. Huh? Now this bug has been with us for so long you'd think they would have something about it in the database, and maybe they do, but half-a-dozen queries brought nothing up. The text I saw gave instructions that appear in the manual but showed no recognition of what can go wrong. Hmmmmm.

Computing Forums

Dedicated to individual topics, the forums listed on the left of the Computing window let you jabber with other obsessives on your favorite software; post complaints and pleas for help; support other members who've gotten confused using similar hardware or software; download and upload speciality items; and take part in the weekly conferences.

In most forums, you'll find a software library (go there to collect software or other files you might want), a message board (for posting to and reading messages from other members), special interest groups within this special interest (such as tiny utilities that strip unwanted returns and tabs out of ASCII text from a mainframe).

You know what you're interested in, so just browse around. You will certainly find some fascinating files, an exchange or two that rouses your ire or pleasure, and, who knows, you might get help on a really critical problem someday—not from the vendor, I expect, but from another member.

CHAPTER **10**

Education

The Education Department acts like a community college—
and high school and grammar school—for America Online.
As in school, there are a career placement office and lots of
rooms devoted to helping you prepare for tests, do your
homework, look up information, and, oh yes, even take
courses. And at the library, there are an awful lot of things
you can look up. You can learn a lot here, but we still
haven't reached the day when all the books in the library
are available, in full text, online. This Department just gives
you a glimpse of that glory day.

Learning

AOL has recruited a lot of teachers to create real courses
online, and they provide plenty of backup, too.

Correspondence School

Click the icon for Correspondence Schools, and you
find yourself in a familiar institution—the International
Correspondence Schools. They are used to provide long-
distance training and they supplement the old-fashioned

course by mail with online classrooms, online bookstores, and question-and-answer learning. You can register for online courses that focus on career development: air conditioning, animal care, art, auto mechanics, basic electronics, bookkeeping, travel agenting, TV repair, wildlife conservation. ICS also offers help in landing a job. But this training takes place, for the most part, on paper; you read something and send in paper homework. For learning online, you should go to the Online Campus.

Online Campus

Listed on the right side of the Education window under T for The Online Campus, you'll find a directory of several different schools delivering courses over AOL.

AOL has created its own set of courses, called Interactive Education Services. These courses are for any age and almost any interest; you get no credit, but you do learn a lot because you study at home, then join a chat session to discuss the material, upload your work, download instructor comments, and get help from other students. Years ago, when AOL was just getting going, I helped put together a course on AppleWorks for Budgeting; since then, hundreds of teachers, hobbyists, and professionals have created online courses. It's a bit weird to sit down in a classroom with no one else there, but once you start chatting, you'll find you are able to follow the ideas just as you would in class, except that you are sitting at your desk at home.

The Electronic University Network offers accredited courses leading to an AA, BA, or MBA. At the graduate level, for instance, you can take Accounting for Management Decisions, Microeconomic Analysis, Quantitative Analysis for Decision Making, and Organizational Behavior. Check out this program if you've been wanting to get some college or graduate courses but can't get out of the house even in the evening.

Support for Parents

Listed on the right, the Parents' Information Network addresses almost any issue you face as a parent: adoption, child abuse, giftedness, home schooling, Montessori approaches, scouting, study skills, substance abuse. Find out what experts say, and temper that with the comments of other people who are struggling just as you are.

A great resource, in the list of Education features, is the reviews of education software. You wonder what to buy, what works, and for what age and temperament. The Education Software sections are arranged by operating system (Mac, Apple, DOS, Windows), and then within that, by course area (math, reading, and so on). You can search the library, look up articles, and get transcripts of discussions.

Support for Kids

Student Access (listed on the right under its sponsor, *The Princeton Review*) is aimed at students, particularly in high school—offering college news, high school news, information about study abroad, support in taking national exams, plenty of reference materials, and some helpful utilities to download. Like most students, this forum views the College Boards as a burden, not a wonderful opportunity to show off their talents. By contrast, the College Board Online takes the party line and helps you get old exams, sign up for new ones, and get ready.

Kids Only Online (KOOL) is aimed at kids from age 6 to 13, with plenty of games, programs, and articles. From the KOOL window, you can get to homework help online.

KIDSNET is a nonprofit organization providing reviews of educational TV and radio shows, plus study guides so you can talk with your kids about the show and get more out of each show. If you want to take advantage of the potential of TV, KidsNet can help. See the similar forum sponsored by National Public Radio Outreach.

Getting out of school at last? Looking for a job? Wondering where to find an employment agency? The Career Center can help you even if you're not a kid, although it's designed to explain the mysteries of résumés, employment agencies, and job listings to first-time job seekers (Figure 10.1). If your son or daughter is about to graduate and needs solid information, this is the place to come. There are profiles of almost every job in the U.S., a library of resources, a list of employment agencies, a list of employers, a list of jobs available (unfortunately, many of these jobs require some experience), and even a list of career guidance services. Live people help counsel you, too.

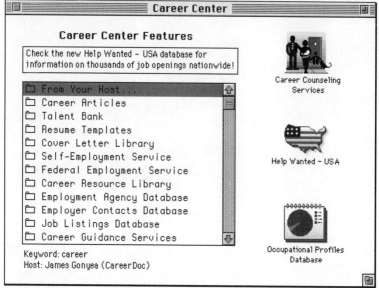

Figure 10.1 *Career Center window*

Support for Teachers

If you're patient, you can learn a lot about what other teachers around the country are doing. Check out the Teachers' Information Network first for plenty of discussion, articles, and support. Then go to the specialty centers, such as the NEA Public Forum, the National Council of Teachers of English, the National Principals' Center, and the Forum on Technology in Education and Training. For research sponsored by the Department of Education and other government agencies, check out Ask ERIC.

For whole lesson plans built around guess-who's video disks, books, online chats, and so on, go to KIDSNET, Scholastic Forum, the National Geographic, and National Public Radio Outreach.

CHAPTER **11**

ENTERTAINMENT

There's a wide range here, from TV and trivia to the *Atlantic Monthly* and best-selling books. Some of the items from other areas show up here, too, if they have some amusement value.

Cartoons

Liven up your in-house memos, decorate your refrigerator, or just download and laugh—most of these are by professional cartoonists, but some are by amateurs (and these aren't a lot worse than the work of the pros). In any given month, some of the subjects are bound to overlap, so you can compare different cartoonists' approaches to the same issues, to see which you prefer.

Right now, Mike Keefe, Modern Wonder, McHumor, Dilbert, and CompuToon are the main contributors. The message board lets you sound off about the funny pages, comic books, editorial cartoons, or anything related to toons. Campaign for or against a strip. A fair number of the participants seem to be artists or cartoonists, but there are plenty of fans, and conscientious objectors.

 Remember that the cartoons come compressed, and that AOL unpacks them on your hard disk after the Download Manager puts them there; you'll need about three times the space indicated, because you have to accommodate the compressed file plus the uncompressed GIF (Graphic Image Format) file. (You can always delete the compressed file later.)

Critics' Choice

This team reviews movies, video discs, books, games, music, and in a few paragraphs tells you what they think. They also run contests, provide whole databases of background on movies, and offer oddball extras such as a postcard from "Twin Peaks" ("Please check your chain saws at the door"). They also post their own wire-service featurettes—one-paragraph stories on breaking entertainment news. The member discussion tends to wander the distance.

Horoscopes

You have to know your sign. If you do, you can open up your horoscopes for the week from the column on the right in the Entertainment window. Find out what your lucky number is for the day (essential for betting the lottery), how bright your financial outlook is, and what the chances are for romance. That's it. There's nothing else here.

La Pub

Here's a chat room designed like "Cheers". You imagine you're in your neighborhood tavern, hangout, or saloon and chat with people who come there regularly. Of course, this bar has plenty of La Hot Tubs available, and the bar is often self-service. Every week you encounter some new contests such as "Spring Break—Tell where the girls/boys are!" and "LateNite Secrets Night...Got any to share?"

La Pub Notes let you celebrate someone's birthday, talk about where to go for vacation, celebrate vegetable pets, and describe imaginary events, such as nearly drowning when doing the belly dance in La Hot Tub.

If you like La Pub, you'll want to go down to the cellar and look at pictures of other people who hang out there, collect tons of bar sound effects (greetings, background noise) if you have speakers ready, or transcripts of various events. In the section devoted to extras (naturally, it's Lagniappe), you'll find utilities for converting sounds from PC to Mac and back, picture viewers, lists of smileys, and even Quick Time movies of members getting ice cubes put down their shirts.

Movies

Click the Movies icon on the main Entertainment window to go to a list of movie stuff. Critics' Choice gives you lots of reviews of movies past and present, ratings lists, competitions, interviews, visits to the Montreal Film Festival—a little of everything, plus a chance to argue with the critics about their opinions. Video Guide is a much skimpier section, offering reviews of just those tapes that are coming out this month.

Hollywood Online (Figure 11.1) lets you sneak into a press briefing on new movies (generally a press photo, but occasionally a short video clip), download photos of stars from the Pictures and Sounds library, read production and cast backgrounders in Movie Notes, schmooze on the Movie Talk message board, and, occasionally, pick up promo posters, passes, and T-shirts for films the producers hope will be blockbusters.

Clicking Hollywood Online's Multimedia button, I found a dozen or so "interactive kits" for Mac and Windows, providing big (no, humongous) files in color that take 25 minutes or more to download at the top speed (9600 baud). Some of these kits are just previews; others offer a little extra info; the ones I tried were all locked, so that I could not grab a frame from the movie to put in a review. (For that, I was forced to rely on the prepared images provided elsewhere.) The multimedia backgrounders for some of these films, hyped as *magazines*, let you flip pages, zip to a topic you want to know about, copy entirely ("Please, please copy," they seem to be saying), and print. Another area offers a few of the Multimedia Tools you might need to display some of these digital ads.

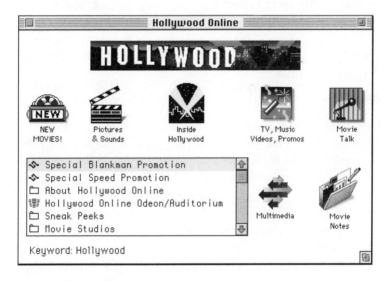

Figure 11.1 *Hollywood Online*

The Movie Notes are just what obsessed fans, or movie critics, need to be able to write a slapdash review. You get the bio, the glare of the spotlight, and in many cases, more details than you ever wanted. Sometimes, though, the bios are revealing. It was fascinating to see how one director went from film school to X-rated porn to R-rated violence to self-proclaimed "films of social importance," which, of course, still retained plenty of bared breasts and exploding buildings. Horatio Alger goes to Hollywood.

Online Gaming Forums

You may have played computer games, in which you compete against the machine, or another person, by alternating
turns. But because there are so many people online, you can
play against a bunch of folks, or one on one against a total
stranger, in fake-medieval fantasy realms, imaginary casi-
nos, or outer space.

Click the Games icon on the left of the Entertainment
window, then double-click the Online Gaming Forums for
play-by-mail, simulation and strategy games.

If you're interested in designing computer or noncom-
puter games, jump into the Game Designers' Forums.

Look up games you are thinking about in the Game-
Base. You can add your own comments.

To talk to representatives of various game companies,
go to Game Company Support.

For a world of dragons, dungeons, and other romantic
notions, open the Free-Form Gaming area. The arena offers
space for up to 200 fighters, spell casters, and thieves; you
can duel with swords or fists. In the Free-Form Gaming
Library you can find pictures of characters with names like
Glorhenath, Rafeki del Armes, and Duzenflika. The message center offers Dragon Tales, a bulletin board in which
you can post brief snippets of Tolkien-like fiction for others
to coo over, with "tales of adventure and daring do, epics of
heroes and villains." Or turn to Red Dragon Innsights for
descriptions of imaginary paintings, classified ads, markets
(welcome to the medieval mall), news, and gossip (Figure
11.2). Sci fi has set up a bar here, too at Stars End.

To chat with people about these games, visit the Red
Dragon's Great Hall, at the top level of the Free Form Gam-
ing Forum; when you get there, you will see that the chat
room is also called the Dreamweavers' Lair. Or go to the
People Connection (Keyword PC) and enter the Red
Dragon Inn, sponsored by the Free Form Gaming Forum.
They describe the inn this way: "It sits at the focal point of

all time and all dimensions, touching upon every world thought of by man and then some. It is the very center and heart of the Multiverse, a sea of Chaos swirling about the Plane of the Red Dragon; a place where hapless Paladins and Cyberboys can meet and drink and tell the strange tales of how they happened upon such a remarkable place . . . and tales of the many adventures they have encountered since arriving at the Red Dragon Inn." You can set up duels, meetings or fights here.

By the way: The Games window offers two other areas: Unlimited Adventure, and Games Parlor. The first is another adventure space with a twist: you can build your own adventures. The vendor, Strategic Simulations, Inc., says "It is more than just a game — UA allows you to develop, design, and play your OWN adventures! UA comes with a complete suite of fantasy artwork and game design tools, making it easy for the most novice of players to become game designers."

The Games Parlor offers online versions of games you might play in your living room.

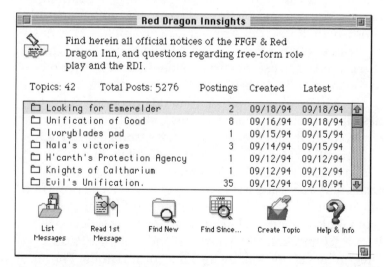

Figure 11.2   *Red Dragon Innsights*

If you want to play but don't have time to commit an evening, or an hour, turn to the Play-By-Mail and Strategy Gaming forum. You can pop in, see what's happening, then sign off and think about it. Later, when you have a move prepared, you can sign back on, post a message with your next attack, and sign off. These Starfleet and chess-by-mail games are alternately quick and slow; ask the Game Master for tips. If the game's been adapted from a regular board game, you'll find a set of the "adapted" rules for online play.

 Windows Users! You can, with the Keyword Casino, get to play poker, craps, and blackjack: First, download some extra software called RabbitJack's Casino (it's free); then, when you run that on your own computer and connect via AOL, you enter a casino, get a bunch of chips, and sit down at the gaming table.

RockLink

Click the Music icon on the left to visit the Nightclub (to chat about contemporary music), check out news from vendors, participate in the Grateful Dead forum, and, best of all, link up with Rocklink, where you can talk with DJs from radio stations and clubs, record reps from major labels, musicians, and other fans. For chats, go to Gossip and pick a genre. Want to know when a concert's scheduled? Wonder how the new tour's being reviewed? Want to see one of the charts? Check Reviews/Charts/Concertline. For transcripts of a lot of interviews, see Rock Interviews.

 Even more than material in other areas, these music-biz sections change dramatically and unpredictably. Most of the names of areas and forums have shifted over the last few months and may do so again. You can find the same functions, but they may appear under new names.

If you're into artists from Warner Reprise Records, they have a whole forum; you can get tour dates, press releases, bios, and other PR. Warner's Multimedia forum is not very multimedia—mostly you get pictures of album covers and publicity shots.

To find out about new releases (and re-releases), click the icon called New Releases. I'm glad to see that the Ramones are reissuing my favorite commentary on sedatives: "Everytime I Eat Vegetables It Makes Me Think Of You." Click the airplane taking off for tour dates (Artists on Tour). Ignore the black-and-white icons scattered around the top—they seem to be for decoration only.

Television

Click the icon for Television and Radio on the Entertainment window. You get a list of topics: NBC online, network shows, TV gossip, TV viewers online, educational TV database, Critic's Choice, soap opera summaries, and, in the directory called More, the National Public Radio Outreach, Discovery Channel, and Learning Channel. (Always click More, to find out what's there!)

If you have an urge to comment on an NBC show, go to their forum, and click Talk to NBC. You'll get a form to fill out and email to them. They make shaky promises to get back to you as quickly as possible. You can order tickets for the live shows, find out who's going to be on upcoming shows, and get all their press releases. If you follow a particular show, click Shows on the right, and you can get star bios, photos, credits, and a history of the show. (The press folks have put at least one picture of every star in their Photo Gallery, as well). You can get local listings, too.

The other networks listed under Networks, and More, show their effort to reach out, and make viewing more interactive and educational (lesson plans based on C-Span!). MTV offers press photos of Beavis and Butthead,

and beachballs at their Lollapalooza location, plus various
graphics tools overadvertised as "multimedia." If your
cable provide Court TV, you should tune in—you get a con-
tinuing legal education, in-depth visits to courtrooms
around the country, documentaries on prisoners, and "stories" put together from footage of famous trials. Yes, you
can see Lorena Bobbitt as she appeared in court. C-SPAN,
too, is doing more than I ever imagined: It has classroom
modules, lots of message boards, ways to order
transcripts—and complete videotapes—in Viewer Services,
and a big bus full of TV equipment that can come to your
school to show how they make broadcasts.

At first, you'd think the Shows forum might have too
much in it. But so far only a few shows have gone to the
effort of posting their schedules. *Geraldo Rivera* is one: next
week, on Monday, Geraldo deals with tales of tormented
twins ("Julie has slept with every one of her twin's
boyfriends. Debra's twin murdered her boyfriend and now
says she's after her."). On Tuesday, women raped by police
officers. On Wednesday, sticky situations: "What would
you do if you came home to find your husband in bed with
your own daughter-in-law?" Thursday brings us the author
of *Radical Honesty.* And Friday, "Women who left their
husbands for another woman." From the messages, I gather
Geraldo ran a show on online sex and got tons of messages,
some people pointing out that they use AOL for something
other than cyberflirtation, some sneering, and some (I
gather) shrieking. CBS removed the ones they thought were
"baseless," but that provoked an even louder outcry. Now
they have a folder called TRASH GERALDO, in which they
bravely accept any kind of criticism. You can also order
show tickets and videotapes ($29.95 each) here.

By the way, the *Ricki Lake* show books the same guests, I
guess. ("We're family but we hate each other.")

Video Games

In the list on the right of the Entertainment window, double-click Video Games. This forum's for you if you run a Nintendo or Sega box off your TV. Get the Game Boy codes here or tips on Mortal Kombat II. Want to cheat? Here's how. You can skip back up to a certain level with these backdoor keys. Find out how to block power bases in the Japanese imports (with Japanese manuals). Or ask Dr. Gamewiz.

 If you have a Windows sound editor, or a program to convert WAV to SND on the Macintosh, you can download many of the sounds from games, as files, and then replay them on your computer. Look in the area called Windows Games WAVs. Hear Toejam and Earl's chickens, snores, and wake-up grunts on your desk!

In the bulletin boards and chat rooms, drool over the specs for Project Reality (more power than a Cray, at less than the cost of a CD-ROM drive, yes, but delivered when???). Ask real developers what computer language to use, how to get started, where to get a job. The Senate has been posturing against violence in computer games, and a lot of members are upset; you can join the campaigns, pro or con. Another folder deals with the whipped-together magazines about video games; one writer suggested the *Game Fan* could be a good magazine if they fired the entire staff and started from scratch by hiring high school graduates who had actually taken English classes.

 For the inside dope on computer-driven games, go over to the Computing and Software area on Apple games (Keyword: AGM), PC Games (Keyword: PGM), and Mac Games (Keyword: MGM).

CHAPTER **12**

Internet Connection

America Online has recently taken most of the headaches out of the process of driving along the infobahn known as the Internet—the grand network of networks, the database of databases, the list of all lists. Through America Online's gateway to the Internet you can send personal messages to people around the world; regularly exchange ideas with people who are interested in similar topics, using a Mailing List; dial in, skim through messages posted by a Newsgroup, and occasionally respond; or use your own Go-fer to look up facts, tirades, and white papers posted on bulletin boards in universities, government agencies, non-profit corporations, and businesses anywhere on the high-tech globe.

Sending Mail over Internet

You can compose a message to someone out on the Internet in almost the same way you compose one to another member of America Online. You choose Compose Mail from the Mail menu, enter an address, and type your message. But you can't attach a file, because files aren't as easy to send as

strings of ASCII characters are. And you must get the
address right. To send Internet mail:

1. **In the Internet Connection, choose Mail Gateway.**

   You see a list of articles giving you tons of advice about
   sending mail on the Internet.

2. **Click the Compose Mail icon on the right.**

   You see the standard form in which you compose AOL
   mail.

3. **Enter the Internet address in the To box.**

   The address has two parts: the user's name, or nick-
   name, or handle, followed by an "at" sign (@), and the
   user's organization. For instance, my user name is Jon-
   Price, and my organization—the organization through
   which I am connected to the Internet—is AOL. The
   organization name must be followed by a period, and
   a suffix explaining what kind of organization it is. For
   instance, a school is .edu, a government agency is .gov,
   and a business is .com. So my full address is:
   JonPrice@AOL.com.

   Generally, if you know who you are sending to,
   you should just ask them for their Internet address if
   they are directly connected, or their username if they
   are on another information service. The first time you
   send a message, place a phone call, and say, "Did you
   get my Internet message?" You need to make sure they
   did receive it, to confirm that you have the address
   down right.

   If you are sending to someone who is using another
   information service, click the Internet Addresses icon,
   to find out how to formulate the address for
   AppleLink, ATT, Bitnet, CompuServe, Connect, Delphi, eWorld, FidoNET systems, GEnie, HandsNET,
   MCI Mail, NBC NightlyNews, Online Career Center,
   Prodigy, Rush Limbaugh, SprintMail, the U.S. Con-

gress, the Well, or the White House. If the person
you're sending to is not at one of those locations, follow AOL's advice in this section on searching for Internet addresses.

4. **Type your message.**

   Do not even try to attach a file.

5. **Click Send Now or Send Later.**

Exploring Newsgroups

Newsgroups are informal groups of people who are interested in the same subject. The members come from schools,
universities, government labs, military bases, small businesses, homes, and almost anywhere there's a phone line in
the wall. Most newsgroups are noncommercial; that is, if
you post an ad, most folks will respond with angry messages, "flaming" you. But if you just read the messages you
find, you will learn a lot about your favorite subject, and,
soon, begin posting your own questions, as well as replies
to other messages.

   Unfortunately, there are so many newsgroups—with
new ones created constantly—that the current list of the
ones we know about would take up most of the pages of
this book. America Online, therefore, has simplified the
process of finding newsgroups you might be interested in.
First of all, they provide you with their selection of top
favorites, and those appear under the icon Read My Newsgroups. Go there first, and delete any that seem too boring
to bother with, so you have room for others. To add a
Newsgroup:

1. **Choose Keyword from the Go To menu, and type
   Internet.**
2. **Click the icon Newsgroups.**
3. **Click the icon Add Newsgroups.**

You see a list of types of newsgroups (Russian Language, alternative, science, recreation, plus organizations such as NASA and Northern Telecom).

4. Select a group of Newsgroups, and click List Topics to see the names of the Newsgroups.

5. Select a newsgroup, and keep clicking List Topics to read some of the messages that have been posted.

6. At the very bottom, when you have reached a single newsgroup you like, click the Add button, to add it to your list.

In a moment, you'll see a message confirming that you have added it to your list.

Of course, the folks at AOL have picked only a few hundred out of the thousands available on the net.

To post a message:

1. From the Internet Center, click Newsgroups, then Read my Newsgroups.

2. Delve into a subject, and get down to the level of messages.

3. Click Send Response, and type your message.

AOL takes care of the incredibly complicated addressing process. You just write, and say "Send it." Soon, if you keep checking the newsgroup, you see your own message appear.

Exchanging Ideas with a Mailing List

Like a newsgroup, a mailing list is an association of people interested in the same topic, whether it is flycasting, hypertext, or cooking. But a mailing list keeps coming at you. If you subscribe, you actually receive every message that is posted on the mailing list, whereas in a newsgroup, you can dial in, read what you want, and exit. Be very sure you want the mail, because you can easily pile up a thousand messages a week, if you subscribe to several popular lists. AOL allows you only 550 messages in your mailbox, and

discards oldest messages first, so if you don't regularly collect your mail you lose personal messages along with the
mailing list postings. To sign up for a mailing list:

1. **In the Internet Center, click Mailing Lists, then click
   Search Mailing Lists.**

2. **In the search dialog that appears, type the subject you
   are interested in, and click Search.**

   A list of mailing lists devoted to that topic appears. If
   nothing shows up, try synonyms. If too many show
   up, try narrowing the field by saying x and y, meaning
   the list must deal with both issues before it is selected.

3. **Save the window that describes how to sign up.**

4. **Follow the instructions, to the letter.**

   Each mailing list has its own signup procedure, which
   depends on the computer system handling the process.

Looking up Facts using Gopher and WAIS

Many organizations have opened up their databases to the
public using applications such as Gopher (it goes out for a
search), WAIS (pronounced "ways," a database standard
developed by Brewster Kahle of Thinking Machines, with
support from Apple, Dow Jones, and KPMG Peat
Marwick). As the people at AOL put it, using Gopher to
browse through menus, submenus, and submenus is like
reading through the table of contents of a gigantic book,
whereas posing a question to WAIS is like skimming
through an index. To search using Gopher and WAIS:

1. **Click Gopher in the Internet Center.**

2. **Double-click any topic that interests you, and then . . .**

   Keep double-clicking the directory icons until you
   reach an actual fact.

3. **If you see an open book, double-click that to perform
   a WAIS search, which may take you to an actual article
   or to additional lists.**

Downloading Files from the Internet

Alas, at the time of my writing, you can't easily do this through America Online. The staff is building the apparatus to make this process seem simple, but in fact it's so complicated, and so packed with problems that they may have to start with a limited number of FTP (File Transfer Protocol) sites, where the process works smoothly, and only gradually expand to include the trickier ones. The biggest problem is that the files exist on dozens of different kinds of computers, in hundreds of different file formats, and passing a file from one operating system to another often deprives it of some crucial bits, turning what was a wonderful graphic into a meaningless stream of ASCII characters.

CHAPTER **13**

KIDS ONLY

Here's a whole section aimed to entertain, educate, and fascinate kids. Some parts have been designed just for kids, and others are, well, duplicates of material that appears elsewhere in America Online. So, exclusive this isn't. But fun it is, mostly (Figure 13.1).

Figure 13.1   *Dinosaurs recommend the Kids Only Department*

Kids' News

Well, it's grown-up news written simply, with
occasional kidtalk thrown in. Reporting on the possibility
of peace in Northern Ireland, the Tomorrow Morning team
editorialized, "This is a very big deal." Of course, the other
lead story in the international arena reported that 60 goril-
las were still alive in Rwanda, despite the civil war.

When you click the Kids News & Sports icon, you get a
chance to pick from various services. Data Times offers a
sports package. Unfortunately, when Ben wanted to find
out whether San Francisco won or not, Data Times pulled
up articles from more than a year ago. What do they think?
Modern kids will settle for something more than a day old?
TIME for kids actually asks kids what they want, what they
like, what they suggest. "No more stuff about mutual
funds!" A big hit in our house is Weather News. When
you open the window, you get a button inviting you to
view the day's weather map; one click, and you see a full-
color map unroll before you. You can download a recent
picture of tropical storms, and compare that with historical
data.

Kids' Games

Yes, I know. You just play these games to keep the kids
interested. But you can steer kids here to get updates on
Swamp Gas, get reviews of software they yearn for, and
post messages to bulletin boards about any software whose
vendor puts up a board. In the best of these, vendor staff
respond within a day or so.

Hobbies and Clubs

I like the bulletin boards best, with whole folders devoted
to horse lovers, animals, model making, "Star Trek", the
environment, astronomy, and stamp collecting. In the Lego
area, one eleven-year-old said he had been collecting Legos
since age 3, and now wanted to build a whole city. Several
people said they'd built cities, including airports, and oth-

ers picked up the idea and did it themselves. One kid
reported, "In my room I have over 22,000 Lego pieces and
about 64 sets. Anyone think these things will ever be worth
something?" Another desperate builder said, "ANYONE
PUT THE MOTORCYCLE TOGETHER I AM STUCK AND
MY MOM BEING A GIRL CANT HELP. CAN YOU."
Luckily, Titan II was able to offer advice.

A major issue is whether or not a kid has his or her own
screen name. Logging in under Mom or Dad's name is
embarrassing enough, but it's also confusing. ("My name
is Ben, but I'm logged in under Maria, but that's my Mom's
name, get it?")

The messages tend to be a little telegraphic, as most
Kids Only users don't seem at ease with typing. But they
get their point across just fine. For instance, one Lego fan
reported, "i have resently gone on a Lego shopping spree
and i have bought over 100 sets of Legos. I already had
over 5000 Legos to begin with. Now i have built a Lego city
consisting of almost all my Legos. My city is 35 and a half
feet long and 20 feet wide it is huge. "

Generation to Generation

Here's a bulletin board set up to encourage talk between
the generations. In the Native American folder, a number
of kids are getting in touch with older folks to learn more
about their culture. One person wrote, "I'd like to talk to
someone about being Cherokee. My grandma was but she
died before teaching me anything about the culture. Can
anyone help me?" Another wrote: HI- im maybe 1/8
Cherokee but my family spent so much time & energy to
cover it up because they would be shut out so now I cant
even trace my ancestors." People share leads, books, tips,
memories.

Several grandparents have told stories, and talked
about the way approaching death has changed their view
of life. And kids sign on with messages like this: "Grandparents are great because they always spoil you and love

you and are very nice. I think grandparents are fantastic.
For instance, my Grandmother and Grandfather took me
and my brother Austin to Weekie Watchie Springs, Florida
as a surprise. We watched an animal show, an under sea
show with live mermaids, and we even got our picture
taken with one of the mermaids!"

One class studying *To Kill a Mockingbird* exchanged
questions and memories with folks who had grown up in
the South in the 30s and 40s. The detailed memories from
real people, I think, confirmed for the kids that the book
was not "just fiction," but true fiction.

Such exchanges show one way telecommunication can
expand our horizon. Even older folks stuck at home can
offer something of their experience to kids, and in turn the
kids' interest and responsiveness shows how glad they are
to get a glimpse out of their own neighborhood, home, or
school.

CHAPTER **14**

MARKETPLACE

Shopping online you can order enough stuff to fill your garage overnight without doing anything more than typing your credit card number a lot of times. From America Online itself, you can get sweatshirts, T-shirts, mugs, software updates, and books. To start, click the Marketplace icon in the Main menu, or use the Keyword Marketplace.

 Marketplace is one of the few departments in which you may have to pay more than your regular AOL fees—usually because you're buying a service in the real world, or asking people to ship you merchandise. I've used these services and have found them perfectly reliable. But if you ever have a doubt, cancel right away; and if you think there's a hesitation or if you get backtalk, call your credit card company right away—they'll go to bat for you.

Things to Buy

Here are some of the other items you can buy online.

Automobiles

Yes, weird as it seems, you can (almost) buy a car over the phone lines. AutoVantage is a service you pay a $49 fee for. For that, you get complete descriptions of new car features, options, sticker and dealer prices, and road tests. You get similar info on used car prices, so you can shop or sell knowledgeably in that field. You can even set up a discount that averages about $2,000 in buying a new car through this service, depending on the model and year; you just have to go down to the dealer and sign the papers. You also get discounts of 10 to 20 percent from national chains doing tune-ups, oil changes, transmission checks, and so on.

Books

Books should be a natural for online sales—at least from the point of view of the vendor. *Books in Print*, the complete listing of currently available books, comes on CD-ROM disks, and so do the lists of titles available through major wholesalers. Even this book is on those databases! Following that general idea, a vendor called READ USA has hooked its own database together with AOL and offers you a discount as well in the Online Bookstore.

But the vendor has not followed this line very far; instead of selling a lot of books, READ USA has picked a few dozen books in each category and posted them. The bias is toward Windows, away from any other operating system, toward the major vendor in each category, and away from competitors. So if you happen to have the most popular software, this is the place to go. If not, you can still place a special order, but instead of getting a discount, you may pay regular rates.

Computers and Software

You can buy computer gear directly from Computer Express, which deals in hardware, software, and gizmos, or indirectly through the PC Catalog, which lists a lot of hardware and software, but sends you to the original vendors for the actual purchases.

Three stores help you buy computer gear over the phone: Computer Express, which deals in hardware, software, and gizmos; Komando, which sells training for different applications; and PC Catalog, which lists a lot of hardware and software, but sends you to the original vendors for the actual purchases.

At Computer Express I found a fairly limited selection, with an emphasis on new products for children. I had the feeling that the manager chooses only the high-profit items.

The PC catalog lists thousands of products, at discounts, but the weird part is you call the original vendor to buy. And there aren't that many vendors. The prices are OK—for middle-of-the road equipment. I'd say, if you aren't already on ten mailing lists for discount mail-order shops, try here.

Everything

Like a mail-order version of CostCo, Price Club, Best, and other warehouse clubs, Shoppers' Advantage (sometimes also known as Compu-U-Store) lowballs the competition on a huge selection of products. For a fairly low membership fee (it varies, creeping up to $39 a year), Shoppers' Advantage gives great discounts on name-brand products (AT&T, GE, Hoover, Jordache, JVC, Magnavox, Memorex, Nintendo, Panasonic, Pentax, Pioneer, Quasar, Singer, Timex, Whirlpool) because this store doesn't have to display the merchandise. They operate out of a warehouse, and they don't even have to deal with the public coming through. You can skim through the information by looking up a manufacturer, or a type of merchandise, or looking through the sections in the imaginary Department Store; you can even get a list of comparable products with prices and features. I'd recommend that you research your purchase beforehand—perhaps using *Consumer Reports*, a magazine featured in this section. The descriptions are detailed, but condensed; you'll do best if you start off knowing more or less what you want.

The store offers baby goods, cameras, car stereos, china, clothing, computers, crystal, exercise equipment, furniture, games, toys, office products, home furnishings, home stereos, household appliances, housewares, jewelry, and major kitchen appliances. I like the Department Store model. I pick an aisle such as Home Stereos, and then answer a series of questions as the "salesperson" narrows down what I want and then offers me a list of whatever models fit my requirements.

On the other hand, if I know what I want beforehand, I can just name the manufacturer, and model number, and go directly to buy it. The price is guaranteed to be the lowest from any manufacturer-authorized outlet. And you can get a refund on the unused part of your membership, if you cancel.

Flowers

You can send one or a dozen flowers overnight—as long as the flowers are orchids or roses from the Flower Shop. It's $50 for a dozen roses, and you get three color choices; for $30 you get one rose in a vase. The orchids come from Hawaii, and the roses from Colorado; there's an extra fee to send orchids to Alaska; it's also extra to send anything just before Valentine's Day.

So the selection ain't very wide. But compared to ordering flowers over the phone through local shops, this is faster, and you probably aren't as likely to get daisies substituted for tulips.

CHAPTER **15**

NEWSSTAND

AOL has pulled together the online versions of many magazines, newsletters, and newspapers on the service, and displayed them in this department (Keyword: Newsstand). That way, if you can't quite recall where you saw the *New Republic*, you can just look it up in the Newsstand. The icons on the outside come and go, depending on who's paying most, I guess, but the list of publications in the middle just keeps on growing. What I like is the mixture. You get anti-advertising folks like *Consumer Reports* debunking claims for fertilizers and radios, next to magazines that, essentially, reprint press releases from anyone, to bulk up their pages. You have the erudite oil paintings of the *Atlantic Monthly* next to the greasy grin of *Road and Track*.

Generally, each periodical gives you a sampling of its articles, a message board to talk to other members about the issues raised, some method for writing directly to the authors, and a subscription form. Occasionally, you'll also find files and programs you can download, and a database or two full of important facts.

Here's where you can hear individual voices against the great white noise of the news industry. In the Wired folder, John Perry Barlow warns against the Clipper Chip—a computer chip that the FBI and National Security Agency want to put into every phone and modem in America so they can listen in. "Of course, trusting the government with your privacy is like having a peeping Tom install your window blinds." And, to keep things easy for the investigators, the government wants to prevent anyone else from inventing a better encryption standard (a way of coding your messages so no one else can read them). This dumbing-down of telecommunications will limit our capability for telecommunicating to the level of the FBI, which considers phone tapping a science. Barlow quotes the government press release on the Clipper as saying that no U.S. citizen "as a matter of right is entitled to an unbreakable commercial encryption product." That's like saying we can't have envelopes that a cop finds impossible to steam open. Barlow foresees a time when the government will have "the automated ability to log the time, origin, and recipient of every call we made, could track our physical whereabouts continuously, could keep better account of our financial transactions than we do, and all without a warrant. Talk about crime prevention!"

If you want to ask questions about your Windows mouse, or the new System for the Macintosh, you might want to look at Family PC, a lively new magazine from Disney and Ziff Davis, or *Home PC*. Home PC, for instance, has an area in the Newsstand (Keyword HomePC). They have an area called Ask Dr. PC, and even his Mom dials in to ask why her HP LaserJet isn't printing. The magazine reprints its stories in whole or in part, offers a separate collection of its reviews, and offers its own searchable database of reviews of children's software. Their software library gives you demos, patches, and interesting files.

Even *Time*, that champion of articles-by-committee, has set up a forum in which editors can talk directly with readers, and they have persuaded some of their cover subjects to come online for discussions. Plus, they focus on personal opinion, such as this one, from Richard Nixon, published the week he died: "Today China's economic power makes U.S. lectures about human rights imprudent. Within a decade, it will make them irrelevant. Within two decades, it will make them laughable. By then the Chinese may threaten to withhold MFN status from the U.S. unless we do more to improve living conditions in Detroit, Harlem and South Central Los Angeles." The auditorium hosts writers, researchers, and opinion-shapers (they even have a debate between John Perry Barlow and the Clipper Chip's main apologist, Dr. Dorothy Denning). The transcripts make these discussions available long after the event. I prefer the online version to the paper version. It's livelier, and you can locate key articles without storing a stack of back issues in your room.

With the periodicals, you get to read many articles from current issues (though sometimes you only get the first few paragraphs); talk with people who've written articles, or been the subject of an article (Billy Graham came on for *Time*); browse through past issues; search for a particular article in the current issue; discuss issues with other readers; send letters to the editor; and subscribe. Each magazine offers extras. For instance, the *Atlantic Monthly* is rerunning its own 19th-century reviews of classics such as *Tom Sawyer*. Here are some choices:

- *Atlantic Monthly*
- Columnists from the Newspaper Enterprise Association
- *Home Office Computing*
- Local newspapers around the country
- *New Republic*
- *PC Novice*

- *San Jose Mercury*
- *Time*
- *Wired*

 To scour back issues of a dozen or more newspapers (*Philadelphia Inquirer, Miami Herald, Boston Globe,* and others), go to the Mercury Center, and choose News Library (Keyword: MC Library). But do this at night, because they charge 10 cents a minute above your regular connect charges. (That's because this is not an AOL service, but a gateway to another service.) You have to pick a paper, a year or range of years, and then type a search word; you get any articles that mention that word, including many that don't really deal with the subject you had in mind. Conclusion: You'll learn most if you ask about local issues, and limit the search to a particular year.

Columnists and Features

The Newspaper Enterprise Association offers a few columns from each of its several dozen columnists, plus a chance to send comments to them, or to comment on other columnists. You can also post pros and cons about Rush Limbaugh, George Will, and other folks who aren't handled by the NEA.

The bulletin boards seem to be a spot in which you can try out your **own** columns, because they accept much longer postings than most places. Check out the X Generation forum in Meet the Columnist. I didn't notice any columnist actually responding in these forums, but the other writers certainly make up for that in noise. You can also have the NEA forward messages directly to its columnists.

Cowles SIMBA Media Information Network

Media about media! The editors scan the wires, do a little interviewing of their own, and then post the top dozen stories in their wrapup, the Media Daily. Pretty wide range: from stories about Microsoft and Apple battling over multimedia, to inside dope about Time-Warner's plans to compete in the online services market.

One reason Cowles can load so much on the net is that it puts out a lot of newsletters, on subjects such as the Electronic Marketplace, Multimedia Business, Book Publishing, and Information and Database Publishing. You can, of course, collect the catalog (see the Products icon), but the forum's a reasonably soft sell. Cowles obviously hopes to impress you with its diligence, and then make it easy to sign up.

Disney Adventures

For kids aged 7 to 14, this magazine explores science, sports, current events, and show biz; it's got comics and puzzles, too. The editors see AOL as a chance to rub elbows with their readers. So they offer a very easy reader survey every month. When I took this, they wanted to know whether I listened to audio books and used a CD-ROM. Yes. And they have two live chats a week with contributors and staffers.

In the Animals folder, you can find out about weird dogs ("Maybe he likes grape juice!") and you can decide if your pet is nuts (probably not).

Alas, no pictures! That absence makes some stories a little hollow: For instance, the Big Adventure tour of the back rooms at the White House shows us where Chelsea likes to do her geography, but, uh, there's no picture. Just the caption. The longer articles, though, are written well for kids, and some are scary and exciting, like the description of treasure hunters and shipwrecks.

If your kids collect baseball cards (or hockey, or Jurassic Park, or POG disks from Passion fruit Orange Guava drinks), there's a forum full of tips on collecting and selling. Pondering careers? Steer kids to the Cool Job folder to learn about worm ranching and designing costumes for Michael Jackson. And then there are contests for best sandwich (the winner will make you barf, they say), best egg, and best scary story. Before leaving, download the Mighty Ducks' logo!

National Geographic

Those rows and rows of yellow magazines have been torn apart and put online—or at least, some of the articles have. The focus here is kids. So the editors who run the online area have taken a few pieces from the magazine itself, and its spinoffs, *Traveler* and *World*, plus press releases and a flurry of projects designed to involve school kids in geography, such as:

- NGS Kids Network: Teachers get lesson plans, handouts, overheads, videotape trainings, and disks for their classroom computers, for students in grades 4 through 6 who are exploring science topics such as weather, water, trash, and solar energy, then swapping ideas with other kids via telecommunications or AOL itself.

- Geographic Interactive: In various formats of CD-ROM and video disk, you can order interactive encyclopedias on animals and presidents. Lots of photos, videos, maps, articles, and timelines, with a pop-up glossary, a game, and a database. Then teachers can order lesson plans, kids can exchange messages about the projects, and you can even download parts of the disk. Kids use all this material to put together reports, then post the reports on AOL for others to read.

- Geographic TV: Schedule of broadcasts, plus teacher's guides, and a full catalog of the hundreds of films and videos available (but you have to call the 800 number to find out how much they cost).

- Ask Geographic: Get some of your questions answered by staffers, and hear what other AOL members think. Collect bibliographies (including an amazing number of their articles) on most subjects assigned in grade school and high school social studies.

The New Republic

Next to in-depth analyses of the Latin American left, you get poems, TRB's sharp skewering of the elite of Washington, and outraged articles pointing out the failings of our government, both at home and abroad. The writing's intelligent, though sometimes smart-ass; the ideas always interesting, even if a bit unrealistic; and you can discuss current topics with angry conservatives, upset liberals, and a few rational beings.

Too bad William Buckley hasn't put the *National Review* up online. But until he does, the right and left can butt heads here.

Windows

If you use Windows, this magazine offers features on subjects such as energy-efficient PCs, plenty of reviews, some how-to's for beginners, a database, and a lot of tips. The advice is tightly compressed but invaluable. If you get an "out of memory" message, for instance, you should run DOS applications on the whole screen rather than in a window; of course, this idea only works in 386 Enhanced mode. How do you switch? Well, that's intuitive: Press Alt and Enter at the same time, or choose full screen in the application's PIF settings. Got that?

You can download some neat utilities, too, such as the U.S. Debt calculator. (Every second, it updates an estimate of the current U.S. national debt and tells you what your share is.) Shareware, drivers, sounds, music, fonts, games, wallpaper, and demos.

For DOS and Windows, see *PC Novice*, *PC Today*, *PC World*, and *Windows*. For the Macintosh see *MacHome*, *MacTech*, and *Macworld*. For computers in general, see *Compute*, *Family PC*, *Home Office Computing*, and *HomePC*.

Wired

You don't get the crazy graphics running every which way under the text (and over it), so the online version is a lot easier to read, though a little blander in style. This magazine hotwires you into the electrosphere, with plenty of rants and raves and talk about networking, internetting, new technology, and cyberpunk.

Conceived of as "the magazine for the digital generation," *Wired* focuses on visionaries like MIT's Nicholas Negroponte, not product ratings; the roots, not just the fruits; ideas, not just announcements. The editors aim to reinvent the magazine article. Here's one of their guidelines for writers: "Write your review. Then write us a letter explaining why we should devote space to your item. Throw away your review and send us the letter." Another: "Amaze us!"

Wired has joined the Electronic Freedom Foundation and other groups in campaigning against the Clipper Chip and other government invasions of privacy via the so-called information highway, which, by the way, includes the Internet and your own membership in America Online. The current FBI position seems to be that they should have the right to look at your e-mail, without a warrant, just to see if anything's going on. They don't think anything on the net should be considered "private"— except their own plans. *Wired*'s campaign is joined by many folks on both sides of the political fence who know a losing cause when they see one. Basically, if you don't want the FBI reading it, don't send it. You're more exposed to government oversight on the nets than using snail mail.

Check out Jargon Watch, in the Electric Word section. Find out what Death Star Villages are, if you live in New Jersey. And learn what the cybercops on AOL can do if you violate the Terms of Service agreement. (Gosh darn, no swearing!)

CHAPTER **16**

PEOPLE CONNECTION

AOL's brightest idea is to provide a way for everyone who signs on to be able to talk to everyone else, all at once, more or less. The People Connection Department, which centers around the Lobby, offers you rooms in which you can talk with almost two dozen other people at the same time, private chat rooms where only you and some close friends can meet, and conferences where you can hear public figures talk and answer your questions.

The Lobby

When you choose to go to the People Connection, you land in the Lobby. You'll see an ongoing discussion among the folks there.

- If you want profiles of the people here, click People, and then double-click a name.
- If you want to know what chat rooms are open, click Rooms. You'll see a list of Active Public Rooms, with an

indication of the number of members in each (Figure 16.1).

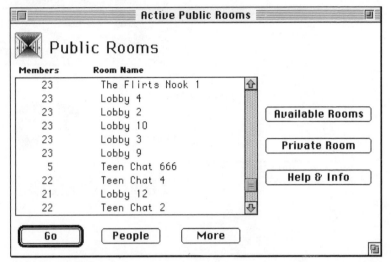

Figure 16.1 *Active Public Rooms*

- For pictures of other members, invitations to romance, games, and lists of events taking place in various rooms today, click the PC Studio.

- If an event is going on in Center Stage, click that, and if there is room, you will be slipped into a row; within the row, you can hear people whispering to each other about the speaker, and then, if you want the speaker to hear you, you can send a message down to the front.

 If the first Lobby gets filled up, AOL creates others, so you can always start out in the Lobby, even if it is Lobby 8.

If you need help, ask for a guide by going to the Keyword GuidePager. They are usually around from noon to 6:00 A.M. eastern standard time weekdays, and all day on the weekends.

Turn to our chapter on Chatting for step-by-step
instructions on how to jump into a conversation.

In the PC Studio, open Romance Connection
(described in Chapter 7) and take a look at the Make
Your Match bulletin boards for people seeking people, or, for the results, the Happy Endings bulletin
board (Figure 16.2). This is the latest version of personal ads, but instead of going to a singles bar, the participants
often go to these boards, or a chat area called La Pub that's been
duded up to look like a bar (Keyword: Lapub), or any of the chat
rooms with names like L'il Flirt.

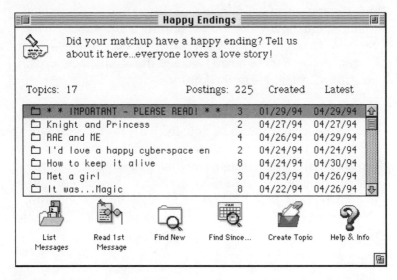

Figure 16.2   *Happy Endings*

Terms of Service

Yes, you should definitely read this section in the PC Studio
to get an idea of all the ways things can go wrong out in the
chat rooms. Basically, AOL will either warn you if they
catch you violating the TOS, or drop you altogether.
According to the TOS, you should not impersonate AOL

staff, disrupt the flow of dialog in a chat room by harassing someone, put a burden on everyone by distributing chain letters, make the screen roll up up up up faster than anyone can read it (just by pressing Return over and over, very fast), or post sexually explicit pictures (defined loosely as showing nipples or genitalia).

Here are some more sins: "The use of vulgar language; inappropriate screen names; committing, or discussing with the intention to commit, illegal activities, is strictly prohibited. Member specifically agrees not to submit, publish, or display on America Online any defamatory, inaccurate, abusive, obscene, profane, sexually oriented, threatening, racially offensive, or illegal material; nor shall Member encourage the use of controlled substances." You can hear that a lawyer has been at work here. But AOL tries hard to enforce these terms, to keep the atmosphere breathable for all members of the family.

Rooms

Out in the rooms, you'll be able to chat about almost any hobby, flirt online (coming close to violating the terms of service, while suggesting more than you say), spot someone interesting and send them an Instant Message suggesting a private chat, and go off to make up your own room. (There are Teen Chat, Thirtysomething, Best Lil ChatHouse, Gay and Lesbian, and Great Outdoors.)

 See Chapter 7 for details on chatting and making up your own rooms.

CHAPTER **17**

Personal Finance

The Personal Finance department focuses on business—
your own finances, your company's ups and downs, and
your country's trade. So you get lots of statistics about
stocks, bonds, and money rates, but you also get a fair
amount of useful advice about careers, investing, economic
trends, and running your own small business.

Money, Money, Money

As the salesman asks on late-night TV, are you really interested in making money? Well, choose the Personal Finance
Department from the Main menu. You'll see a long list of
forums on the left, with various icons on the right, advertising, for instance, Morningstar Mutual Funds (the money
bag) and the latest stock quotes (the arrow going off the
chart). Keyword for this department: Finance.

To catch up on business news, click the icon for Financial News over on the left. You get access to the business
pages of the *San Jose Mercury*, *Chicago Tribune*, and *New York*

Times, and summaries of business, commodity, market, and world trade news. The Business News picks up the latest stories about company earnings, personnel changes, and new product introductions. You can look up by industry, or through a search for a particular company.

For the New York Stock Exchange, American Stock Exchange, Dow Jones, and Standard and Poor's indexes, open the Market News folder in the Financial News section (or use the Keyword Market News). You can find out how the markets are doing in general, or what the top 20 stocks were doing 15 minutes ago, if the market's still open.

 You can't use this system to get the latest quotes on a stock that's not in the top 20. For that, click the Quotes and Portfolio icon on the Personal Finance window. Keyword: Quotes. You can enter the stock's symbol and get a fifteen-minute-delayed quote; you can also list the stocks in your portfolio, with their purchase prices, and AOL will automatically update their prices, so you can see if you are ahead or behind.

Company Stories

Go to Hoover's Company Profiles in the list of Financial Resources on the right, then, from the many services offered by the Hoover folks, choose Company Profiles in that forum. (Keyword: Company). Or just click the icon on the left for Hoover's Company Profiles. You get the data that's printed in the *Hoover's Handbook* reports, including:

- A history of the company, with the names of the founders
- The name and salary of every key officer
- Their address, telephone number, and fax number (at least for the head office)
- Where they operate

- Divisions and subsidiaries
- What they sell
- Their competitors

You can cruise through the listings by industry, country, or just go through the alphabetical list. If you can't recall the company name, try a product, or a person's name, using the Search (Keyword: Hoovers).

Meet the Boss

In the Investors Network, you can take part in discussions about stocks and bonds, hot new companies, or sagging old ones.

You can find out how many ways the IRS has changed its mind about taxes, learn methods of charting stocks and bonds, get reviews of investment software, and get samples of too many financial newsletters.

If you'd like to listen in as the analysts at major mutual funds and brokerages grill the chief executives of companies around the world, choose the International Corporate Forum (Keyword: ICF) in the list on the right or The Personal Finance window. The conferences investigate a few dozen companies in half-a-dozen areas (regional banks, Mexican corporations, biotech, software and computer services) in the course of two or three days; if you miss the interaction, you can get full transcripts, plus supplementary materials, afterward.

To prepare for the conference, read the Prepared Remarks for PR flack plus details about soon-to-be-released products, check the Conference schedule, and submit questions via the forum. The forum staff picks the 20 best questions relating to investment in the companies, posts those the day of the conference, and then you join the VIPs at the Corporate Forum, or collect the transcript in the archives later.

Microsoft Small Business Center

Here's what more software companies ought to do: provide advice, seminars, resources, utilities, and conferences for their customers. Instead of contenting themselves with an explanation of how to use Excel, Microsoft teams up with two dozen other organizations such as the U.S. Small Business Administration, the U.S. Chamber of Commerce, and the American Management Association, to help us with the actual work we bought Excel to do: budgeting, planning, forecasting, tracking inventories, and so on. The pitches are softsell and can be easily sidestepped. Keyword: Small Business.

In this area, you'll find:

- A company that will set you up as a corporation for $115
- A template for your company sexual harassment policy
- Details on how to get a loan from the Small Business Administration
- Advice on getting good publicity locally and nationally
- Contacts with retired executives who will coach you as you develop your business
- Conversations between consultants, public speakers, newsletter publishers, and other freelancers
- Centers that offer women entrepreneurs woman-to-woman help

Consumer Reports

Look up the latest reports on new cars, washing machines, TVs, and stereos. Read new columns. Get access to the toughest evaluations of new products available today.

Worth Magazine

Worth Magazine posts some of its current articles (the best are by former mutual fund manager Peter Lynch), plus answers to questions like these:

1. Do I really need a financial plan?
2. Do I need to go on a budget?
3. How can I find the right financial adviser?

You can download the answers whenever you want. The advice is reasonable, although some is six months old, which may invalidate part of it.

Your Money

Find out how to refinance, how to hire a financial planner—or do it yourself. Run by a certified financial planner, the forum discusses credit; debt; planning for college, estate, or retirement; scams to watch out for; and insurance. Allridge also answers FAQs (those questions that are asked so frequently that most forums don't bother answering them any more) such as, "What's the P/E Ratio I hear so much about?" Answer: "A P/E or price to earnings ratio is the price of a stock divided by its earnings per share. It provides investors an idea of how much they are paying for a company's earning power."

Morningstar Mutual Fund Information

Click the icon of a bag of money. People pay almost $400 a year to subscribe to this service, which offers incredibly thorough analysis of the way 3,400 mutual funds are performing, with critiques of the managers and operations (Keyword: Morningstar). If you haven't studied the stock pages, the statistics here won't mean much to you, but if you have some idea of what a Price/Earnings Ratio is, you'll have a wonderful time asking Morningstar to name its top 25 mutual funds, based on performance over the last ten years; or the best earners in the aggressive growth field, based on the last five years' figures; and you can look up any one fund and get the numbers, estimated risk, and rating (without the little essays that come with the newsletter itself).

This is a good place to list your current mutual fund investments (your portfolio), then dial in every once in a while to see how they are doing. The system calculates your profit or loss (Keyword: Quotes).

CHAPTER **18**

REFERENCE DESK

AOL has had a great idea here. It has collected some 50 searchable databases from the whole online world and brought them together in a single list so you can methodically check out a topic in the *Atlantic Monthly*, the Bible, and *Bicycle Publications*, if you think all three might have something of interest. In addition, they've added Mr. Gopher, the icon for searching directories all across the Internet, using a surprisingly friendly shell.

The Bible

You can look up any word in the Bible, and get a list of all the places it occurs; when you pick one, you get a whole chapter, so you can see the word in context. You can also visit the ethics and religion bulletin boards, which deal with Christian doctrine, Judaism, Buddhism, Hinduism, Islam, and that most famous of all religions, New Age. And there are libraries with software, sermons, and text files about the same subjects; in the Buddhism Library, for instance, you can find free books, learn Tibetan, download the Mani padme Hum prayer, and participate with 106 other contributors in a discussion of Emptiness versus the Void.

Bulletin Boards outside of AOL

You can search for a neighborhood bulletin board, in the Bulletin Board Services database. This database lists thousands of bulletin boards run by individuals or organizations, and gives you help on dialing in.

Compton's Encyclopedia

Click the icon for *Compton's Encyclopedia* in the Reference Desk window, and then choose Search Encyclopedia Articles. You'll get a form in which you type the topic you're interested in; then click List Articles. If your topic's a candidate for a school report anywhere from first through twelfth grade, you're likely to get some "hits," and even at a higher level, you'll get a fairly detailed view of the subject. You'd think that 5,000 articles would just about blanket the world, but they don't; so, although these searches may help your youngsters do reports, you'll often find only a note or two.

Health

The Health and Medical Information area provides an enormous amount of information on wellness, mental health, addiction, sexuality, parents' rights, health reform, children's health, seniors' health, alternative medicines, disabilities, and caretaking (Figure 18.1). For instance, the Home Medical Guide, an icon within the window, lets you figure out whether that sprain is more serious than you thought, double-check your medications, learn about the surgery you're about to undergo, and even find out about rehab devices. For many people with disabilities, America Online offers a rare chance for social contact, and a way to meet and chat with other people who face similar challenges.

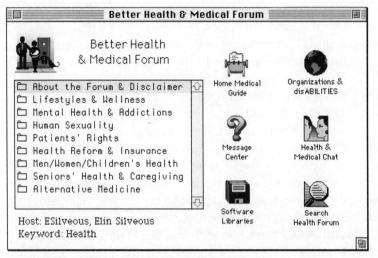

Figure 18.1 *Icons offer information, chats, and bulletin boards full of messages, files, and software about health issues.*

Utah

Several states such as Massachusetts, Michigan, and Utah have set up forums on AOL. The idea is business—and tourism is big business. Utah, for instance, lists licensable technology developed in its many "labratories" as the governor calls them, and advertises its many "Valuable and Unique resources and programs." If you want to make a film there, the Film Commission wants to help; if you want to relocate, the welcome mat is out; and you can learn about recreation (Bear Lake, Flaming Gorge, and Old Deseret), Utah for kids, and Utah arts, as well as the state's universities and colleges. In a few years, I guess, every state will have its own forum.

Washington Week in Review

Here's a show that offers transcripts (Florida Political Factors in Clinton's Cuba Policy), pictures of the staff, local listings, and a weekly trivia quiz on American history (Figure 18.2). Capital Facts offers current names and addresses for people in federal departments, the Supreme Court, and Congress. If you know your Congressperson's name, you can look it up in the House of Representatives list, but if you want to know who goes to the House from your state, well, you have to look in the Senate folder, where they list each state, and tell you who you sent to the Senate and House last time around. Odd way to get there, but useful if you still write letters to your representatives. The Visitor Information, too, is mostly accurate; for instance, they give the right address for the Federal Mint (here known as the Bureau of Engraving and Printing) but don't tell you that you have to go to another address to get tickets. The American History section offers a dozen short documents such as the Mayflower Compact of 1620 and the Virginia Declaration of Rights of 1776—a great idea, but just a beginning.

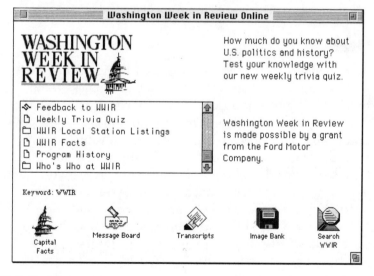

Figure 18.2   *Here's a show that helps you communicate with your political representatives—and encourages you to visit Washington, D.C.*

The Whole Shebang

Here's the current list of databases, so you can get a sense of the range and variety. You'll recognize many from other departments.

AOL Directory of Services
AOL Local Access Numbers
AOL Member Directory
Ask ERIC
Atlantic Monthly
Barrons' Booknotes
The Bible
Bicycle Publications
Bicycling Magazine
Bulletin Board Services
Business Information
Career Center
Celebrity Cookbook
Chicago Tribune
Children's Software Information
Claris Support Information
CNN Newsroom Guides
College Handbook
Columnists & Features
Compute Magazine
Computer Terms Dictionary
Computing/Software Companies
Court TV
C-SPAN
Dining News and Reviews
The Discovery Channel
Disney Adventures Magazine
Educational Magazines
Educational TV & Radio
Environmental Information
GameBase
Geoworks Information
Health & Medical Information

Homeowners' Information
The Learning Channel
Massachusetts Forum
McLaughlin Group
Media Information
Michigan Forum
Microsoft Knowledge Base
Mobile Office Magazine
Movie and Video Reviews
Mutual Funds
National Alliance for the Mentally Ill
The New Republic
Newsbytes
News Search
New York Times
Parenting Information
PC World
Pictures of the World
Popular Photography Magazine
San Jose Mercury News
Scientific American
SciFi Channel
Smithsonian Online
Stereo Review
Television Information
TIME Magazine
Travel Advisories
Travel Holiday
Travel Profiles
Utah Forum
Washington Week in Review
White House Information
Windows Magazine
Wine Ratings
Wired Magazine
Worth Magazine

CHAPTER **19**

Sports

All right, listen up. You know who you are. If you join the football pool at work and cite averages of baseball players most folks have never heard of, you need the Sports department. Whatever's in season gets an icon, leading to game summaries, stats, signings, and odds. Get today's schedule and the latest scores.

Grandstand

Swap gossip about almost every kind of sports in the Grandstand (Figure 19.1).

Starting in the scrolling list on the left, you can visit the Dugout to talk baseball, bounce off the Glass to chat basketball, enter the Squared Circle to fight about boxing, go to the 50 Yard Line to bump heads with football fans, get out on the Green to whisper about golf, shave ice at the Blue Line to hipcheck each other about hockey, get to the Post on time to swap inside tips on horse racing, take your shoes off and enter the Dojo to talk martial arts, slip on into the Pits to chat about auto racing, or visit the Chalet for an aprés-ski

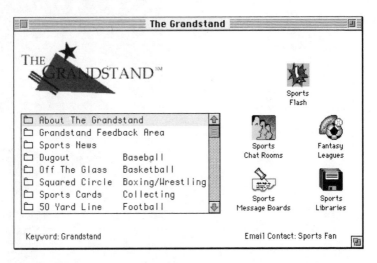

Figure 19.1   *The Grandstand*

discussion of winter sports. Each of these areas offers bulletin boards and chat rooms; most also offer news of the sport, and some kind of files in their software library—photos of stars, the rules, logos of your favorite teams, patches and updates to relevant software, even the team song.

If you prefer to go straight to the chat rooms, click the icon for Sports Chat Rooms. And if you just want to get to the message boards, click the icon for Sports Message Boards. Just want files and software? Click the Sports Libraries in the Grandstand window.

If you want to know what sports personalities may be visiting various chat rooms this week, click the Sports Flash icon.

Like putting together historical players on imaginary teams? Click the Fantasy Leagues icon.

Sports Reports

A company called Data Times clips local papers' stories on many professional teams, then relays them to you. If there aren't many current stories, you get the ones left over from last year. Basically, this so-called service is a rehash.

If you live far away from your favorite team, and don't get their local paper, though, you may want to dial in to get that old nostalgic kick.

Sports News

Here's another section that offers info about sports. Its Scoreboard section contains the kind of game summaries invented when it was expensive to send a telegram; not sentences; tight; guess if you want to fill in blanks. Ok? OK. Not very graceful. The amount of info depends on the day of the week. On a Friday, for instance, you get only one piece of information in the college football section: Virginia Tech beat West Virginia. The NFL Football section contains a replay of the same finals as above (the telegrams), plus Vegas betting odds. Today, your bookie will be expecting the San Francisco 49ers to beat the New Orleans Saints by 15 points. If you're addicted to gambling, though, you have to log off AOL to place your bet by phone. You also get a schedule for the season, but you have to be a genius to figure it out; unfortunately, the creators set up some kind of two-column arrangement, where you start each column with a team, and see their previous wins and losses below—but once that text goes through the telephonic grinder, nothing lines up with anything else, and every abbreviation is in all-capital letters. Ditto for the statistics. I guess all this data is great for cub reporters, but now I see what a service the newspapers do when they reformat this mess in readable form.

CHAPTER 20

Today's News

So this is where you come for the latest news of the world (Keyword: News). Like the old ticker tape rooms in radio stations and newspapers, this department updates all recent stories every few hours, and if you don't have CNN on all day, you can learn about the big and the not-so-big events before your neighbors do.

Click the top button on the Main Menu: Today's News (Figure 20.1). You get a list of hot stories, and then sections devoted to the US & World, Business, Entertainment, Sports, and the Weather.

If you're looking for stories on a topic that might span domestic politics, global issues, and business, try Search News. Type your topic in and click List Articles. If the subject's hot, you'll get a lot of articles; if not, few or none.

Front Page News

From some of these forums, you can see the top two inches of whatever events the editors have decided are the most important stories of the hour. No depth here. This is more like the five minutes of news between blockbuster shows during sweeps month on TV. Often the top news story appears next to an icon on the Welcome screen; clicking the icon takes you to the Today's News list of articles, with that story highlighted.

Figure 20.1 *This department brings together front page stories, and news from areas such as Business and Entertainment.*

You generally get nine or ten paragraphs—equivalent to a local newspaper's story on the subject. This is wire-service prose: clear, balanced, impersonal.

The Rest of the News

Beyond the Today's News stories, you can get more articles, though not necessarily a lot more depth, in directories devoted to the U.S. and World, Business, Entertainment, Sports and the Weather. How's this experience different from reading your local paper?

Well, if your paper's like the *Albuquerque Journal*, the *New Haven Register*, or the *Honolulu Advertiser* (some of my former "hometown" papers), you'll find more information online, representing a more even-handed approach to foreign stories. You can pick and choose more easily just because you don't even see the other stories, and you make a decision on the headline alone—in my case that means I skip more stories.

What's missing? The in-depth local stories (why the Rio Grande is running out of water; the impact of Japanese investment on Hawaiian hotels). The editorials. The cartoons and pictures. And, of course, the local car ads!

The net effect resembles the news summaries handed to the president by the CIA: no nonsense, and not much fun, either. I'd say it's better to turn on CNN for half an hour. (In a few years, of course, you'll be able to download outtakes from TV broadcasts, but right now you're still looking at text, text, text.)

Around the World

This forum collects stories by location, with sections abut Africa, Asia, Europe, the Middle East, Russia, and South America, and then, that strangest of exotic locales, Washington, D.C.

Business

You could find most of this news over in the Personal Finance section, but if you prefer getting all your news in one dose, you can learn about company actions, finances, personnel changes, and updates on the commodities business, the retail trade, media and leisure industries, and finance. Curiously, manufacturing, service, and farming don't rate areas of their own.

Entertainment and Sports

These buttons take you to recycled news from the Entertainment and Sports departments. You could look it up there, as Ring Lardner used to say.

Weather

The most important news of all! Look at yesterday's weather map, radar images, and satellite images; check on the progress of tropical storms and hurricanes; study recent highs and lows, and get the forecasts for U.S. cities.

On the bulletin boards, you can gasp at Mount Washington's new lows, ponder the monsoon season, and point to the ozone hole. These postings remind me of sitting around the Ben Franklin stove in the general store in Appleton, Maine, years ago, saying "Ayup," and "Nosuh," as the old-timers recalled blizzards of '39 and earlier.

CHAPTER **21**

TRAVEL

The big airplane nudges beyond the silhouette of the word Travel. This department will help you plan vacations, and weekend jaunts, make reservations, in fact, do everything but go (Keyword: Travel). You'll see a big list on the right, with half a dozen icons on the left (Figure 21.1).

This is a very chatty area, full of questions from folks about to take off wondering, at the last moment, what to do when they get somewhere. But then there are also a lot of folks who've been there before, know what to do, and where to stay.

The services, here, are professional; in fact, if you were a travel agent, you'd be using these services every day at work. So if you're willing to do some digging of your own, you're likely to outdo the average travel agent, and have a lot more fun on your next trip, thanks to all the travel info here.

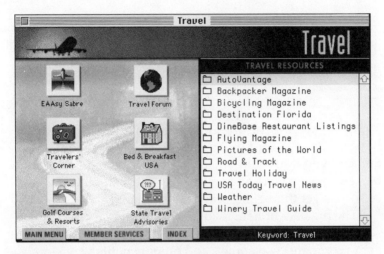

Figure 21.1 *The Travel Department window*

Airline and Hotel Reservations

You can book airline, hotel, and rental car reservations through American Airlines' EAASY/SABRE system. You have to go out through a gateway to this system because it runs on American's own computers, and naturally, it often suggests American's flights first. But it does know about the flights of 350 other airlines, the rooms in 27,000 hotels, and cars at 60 rental companies around the world; and if you just keep scrolling, you can locate any flight, room, or car.

But the interface stinks. No graphics, no menu system— you have to respond to SABRE using its commands, all of which start with a slash. This system is what travel agents use, and even after the training class, they find it hard to navigate, using it every day. As a casual user, you'll find it frustrating, though potentially more helpful than your own agent.

Consider using the EAASY/SABRE help desk: 1-800-331-2690, from 8 A.M. to 8:30 P.M. central time, 9 A.M. to 5:30 P.M. on Saturdays and Sundays. (If you live in Dallas, the number is metro 355-2936.)

By answering the questions in plain English (you don't have to say LAX for Los Angeles), you locate a flight, hotel, and car; you then "join up" by giving your credit card number, and you get a confirmation of a reservation. In a week or so you get the airline tickets in the mail.

The big benefit here is comparison: The process at first seems tedious, but you do find out all the flights, and you get to compare costs, times, and other benefits very closely.

Destination Data

Click the suitcase on the Travel window to go to the Travelers' Corner. Arnie and Beth Weissmann took a tour around the world and found there weren't many up-to-date descriptions of the places people want to go. To fill the gap, they created their Travel Reports, which form the heart of this area; they hire correspondents around the world to update more than 50 destinations every quarter. Each report starts with a snapshot of main attractions, pinpointing who ought to go there, and who ought not to; that's followed with a what-to-do-there section, covering 9,000 cities, plus do's and don'ts, and fascinating trivia. I tested some of the destinations I know personally, and found the text true and savvy.

You can post questions on the Exotic Destinations Message Center for answers from other members and staffers at the Weissmann Travel group; of course, the destinations don't have to be much more exotic than bed and breakfasts in London.

For tips about special deals, discounts, and steals, click the Travel Holiday icon in the Travelers' Corner window and read condensed versions of articles from this magazine. Arthur Frommer, the original budget travel maven, pens a column on items such as a special Hawaiian holiday (one week in Waikiki, with airfare and hotel, if two go). You'll also find rundowns of the newest camera gear, books, and bags.

Travel Tips and Information

Click the Travel Forum in the Travel window and you'll see a hidden valley in AOL: a thousand facts about currency exchange, electricity abroad, European rail passes, insurance, packing, passports, regional airline fares, tips from other travelers about almost any destination, and ways to save money on airfare (Figure 21.2).

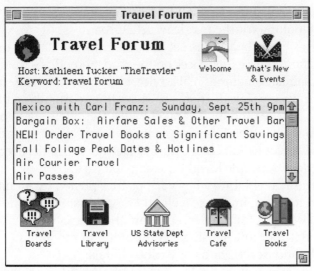

Figure 21.2   *The Travel Forum*

If you just want to get up and go, explore the Air Courier folder in the list at the left of the Travel Forum Window; you get a call, rush out to the airport a few hours before takeoff, and only get to take a carry-on bag because the courier service uses your baggage allowance for a customer shipment. This isn't smuggling; you are taking time-sensitive documents through to avoid delays in customs. The fare's not free, as you might have expected; but it's half of the lowest fare available to the public. You're most likely to get a gig going to somewhere not very popular, in the off-season.

If you want to compare airlines for promptness, baggage losses, and customer satisfaction, open the Air Travel Consumer Report. I learned that in June 1994, Southwest Airlines came out on top of some key categories, with more arrivals on time, more departures on time, fewer reports of lost or mishandled luggage, and fewer complaints per hundred thousand passengers, but Southwest fell behind in bumping ("Involuntary Denied Boardings," almost a routine at the airline). For tips on discounts, read the Bargains folder, learn about Consolidators, and skim through other areas looking for the magic word *Discount*.

The Travel Boards are set up for members to talk to members about their experiences on the road. Sometimes there's complaints, sometimes real advice, and sometimes just stories (see Travelers' Tales). There are 41 postings currently in the Nude Beaches and Nude Travel folder. Definitely check out the Amtrak folder: lots of raves for train travel, particularly from Denver to Salt Lake City and Denver to Seattle; even with delays, people loved the excursion trips.

The Travel Library has various files posted by members about teaching in Japan, Iceland ("You Must See It Once!"), Disney World for Singles, software that tracks your frequent-flier miles, using a computer and modem in hotels, and descriptions of various hotels.

Click the icon of the U.S. State Department to get the latest warnings about travel. Just as American troops poured into Haiti, I checked, and got a bureaucratic caution against visiting Haiti, followed by an explanation of why the text had changed from the week before, when our president was threatening to invade. "This replaces the Travel Warning dated September 15, 1994, to delete a reference to armed intervention and to add information on the multinational force deployment." I always feel better when I am watching a multinational force deployment on TV, rather than on site.

The Travel Cafe invites you to come in, take off your backpack, pull up an espresso and type your chat. You may also visit, more formally, with guests such as Carl Franz, author of *The People's Guide to Mexico.*

The Travel Books icon leads to a list of reviews. The reviewers like the books I like: *The People's Guide to Mexico, Insight Guides,* the *Let's Go* series. Only problem: This is a short list. They ought to add Ray Riegert's *Hidden Hawaii* and the rest of his line from Ulysses Press. Get them today!

CHAPTER **22**

Member Services

This department offers help and comfort to the confused and outraged. Because the AOL customer support people think you're trying to recover from some problem their service may have inadvertently caused, there's no charge for the time you spend in this department. Bravo!

You should dedicate 10 or 15 minutes to exploring this department when you don't need help so you're familiar with it when you do. Just type the Keyword: Help.

So that you don't accidentally run up charges while using support, AOL closes active chat windows and gateways to other services. When you see the message telling you this, just OK it. You see the Member Services window open in the free Help Area (Figure 22.1).

Getting the Answers

Over the years, the support team has answered the same questions over and over. They have written down those answers, and you can get them at the click of an icon.

Figure 22.1   *Member Services*

- If you aren't sure what a command might do, click Menu Bar Help.

- If you have trouble connecting, but your modem and phone lines still work, use the Technical Support bulletin board, at 1-800-827-5808. (Set the telecommunication software to 8 data bits, 1 stop bit, and No parity).

- If you can't get your modem to work with your software, or if you just can't seem to get online, call the telephone support line 1-800-827-3338. You can get prerecorded solutions 24 hours a day, 7 days a week, but you can reach a human from 9:00 A.M. to 2:00 A.M., Eastern time, Monday through Friday, plus 12 noon through 1 A.M. Eastern, on Saturday and Sunday.

- If you would like something on paper, call 1-800-827-5551 and punch through the menu options until you find one that sounds like your problem, type that number, and give your fax line. You'll get the answer on paper in a few moments.

- If you'd like to post a problem and get help from other

members, click Members Help Members in the Member Services window. Look for a directory that might deal with your kind of challenge.

- If you are already online and want to give a full description of your problem to the staff, click EMail to the Staff, and send them a detailed note.
- If you have a billing question, click Billing Information.
- If you have a question about passwords, or parental control, click Account Security.
- If you have a question that hasn't been answered by any of these other methods, click Tech Live Support.

Some of the most requested answers show up in the scrolling list on the left (how to create a screen name, how to change your password). Look here for answers to questions such as:

- What are the access numbers I can use when I am on the road, in Tucumcari, or Timbuktu?
- How can I control my kids' use of chat rooms?
- When does AOL plan to take the system "down" for maintenance or repairs?

When you choose to ask for Tech Live Support, you can count on a little give and take as you ask questions. When you click the icon, the staff responds with a description of the service. Click Tech Live. The staff warns you that if you want to know about other software, you ought to go to Computers and Software; but you don't; so click Tech Live again. Then, if you're online between 9:00 A.M. and 2:00 A.M. weekdays, or noon to 1:00 A.M. weekends, Eastern Standard Time, choose Tech Live Auditorium. Read the blurb, which explains that you should move to row 1-10 for a problem with service, and rows 11-20 for a system error or connection problem. (The idea is that you are sitting in a row with other members, while a staffer walks up and down, answering several questions at once.) Then get in your row and type your question. It may take a few minutes for the staffer to get to you, but when he or she does respond, you'll get an answer you can act on.

Other hours, or for other kinds of questions, click Members Help Members, post your question, and get a lot of feedback from other folks who may have had the same problem.

You can see that this support area has been set up to answer most questions before you take the drastic step of typing to a live human being. Be considerate. If you think your question may be so basic, or so common, that there already is an answer up on one of the areas, look for it before going to the Tech Live Auditorium.

When all else fails, or when you absolutely can't even connect to use the Member Services, call 1-800-827-6364, and you'll reach a very patient human being who will talk you through the solution and make sure it really works before hanging up.

Overall, AOL's customer support is among the best in the business. You have a lot of ways to get help, and when you need a quick response, you'll get it. Companies like Apple, IBM, and Microsoft should study the way AOL does it!

CHAPTER **23**

Resources

Most of what you need to know about America Online is in this book, or crammed into the online help and member-to-member messages.

But if you get into difficulties, try the online help and the Members' Online Support department. But if you just can't make the connection or nothing seems to address your particular problem, call America Online at 1-800-827-6364. That's the general-purpose Customer Relations line. The people who answer the phones form one of the world's best customer support teams. You **will** get an answer!

About the Whole Wide Wonderful Online World . . .

If you'd like to learn more about the online world in general, I recommend:

- *Wired* (the magazine). Keyword: Wired. Virtually the best, latest, hippest, and most outrageous news about everything online (not just AOL). Get the paper version! You can subscribe by e-mail at *wired.com*; by phone at

1-800 SO WIRED, or if you are calling from outside the U.S., 415-904-0660; or by mail at P.O. Box 191826, San Francisco, CA 94119-9866.

- *Online Access* (the magazine). Step-by-step through Internet, and a wide range of online services, including news about America Online. By mail: 900 N. Franklin, Suite 310, Chicago, IL 60610.

About America Online and Similar Services

To get another perspective on America Online, check out Tom Lichty's *Tour Guide* (in Mac or Windows flavors) from Ventana Press.

To find out more about the Internet (the network that surrounds all other networks), read *The Internet Companion*, 2nd ed., by Tracy LaQuey and Jeanne Ryer, from Addison-Wesley. Call 1-800-447-2226.

If you're interested in a very comprehensive book on all facets of the online world, see *The Online User's Encyclopedia: Bulletin Boards and Beyond,* by Bernard Aboba, from Addison-Wesley.

And for guides to competing online services, see Addison-Wesley's other Trail Guides:

The Trail Guide to CompuServe, by Robert R. Wiggins and Ed Tittel.

The Trail Guide to Prodigy, by Caroline M. Halliday, available in February, 1995.

For an exhaustive study, see *A Directory of Electronic Mail !%@::Addressing & Networks,* by Donnalyn Frey and Rick Adams, published by O'Reilly & Associates, Inc.

INDEX

Your Road Map For The Information Superhighway— America Online®

Start Your Test Drive Today!

Before you can exchange ideas with people around the world, you have to learn your way around the information superhighway. No problem. Just go to our Internet Center—your road map to the Internet. You'll find we've made it as easy to handle as America Online. With a point and click, you can access newsgroups on hundreds of topics, send e-mail to other online services or overseas, access information on everything from home brewing to NASA news using Gopher and WAIS databases—and more.

Try America Online For Ten Hours FREE!

Plus, check out America Online's software libraries with over 100,000 files to download. Multi-file downloading and 9600-baud modem access make it fast and easy. You can join online clubs for your favorite hobbies. You can even talk with other members in live conversations, conferences, and classes. All on the most "clickable" online service there is. So hit the information superhighway and head for America Online. It's easy. Simply call 1-800-827-6364, Ext. 3767, to order today!

1-800-827-6364, Ext. 3767